LUCID DREAMING

THE PATH OF NON-DUAL DREAM YOGA

LUCID DREAMING
THE PATH OF NON-DUAL DREAM YOGA

Realizing Enlightenment through Lucid Dreaming

- SERENADE OF BLISS BOOK 3 -

SANTATAGAMANA

Copyright © 2020 by SantataGamana
All rights reserved.
1st Edition, September 2020

ISBN: 979-8683879341

No portion of this book may be reproduced in any form, including photocopying, recording, or any electronic or mechanical methods, without permission from the author except for brief quotes.

Editor: Eric Robins

Disclaimer for Legal Purposes

The information provided in this book is strictly for reference only and is not in any manner a substitute for medical advice. In the case of any doubt, please contact your healthcare provider. The author assumes no responsibility or liability for any injuries, negative consequences or losses that may result from practicing what is described in this book. Any perceived slights of specific people or organizations are unintentional. All the names referred to in this book are for illustrative purposes only, are the property of their respective owners and not affiliated with this publication in any way.

Read also, by the same author of this book:

REAL YOGA SERIES

— KRIYA YOGA EXPOSED
The Truth about current Kriya Yoga Gurus & Organizations. Contains the explanation of Kriya Yoga techniques, including the Final Special Kriya.

— THE SECRET POWER OF KRIYA YOGA
Revealing the Fastest Path to Enlightenment. How Fusing Bhakti & Jnana Yoga into Kriya will Unleash the most Powerful Yoga Ever.

— KUNDALINI EXPOSED
Disclosing the Cosmic Mystery of Kundalini. The Ultimate Guide to Kundalini Yoga & Kundalini Awakening.

— THE YOGA OF CONSCIOUSNESS
25 Direct Practices to Enlightenment. The ultimate guide to Non-Duality (Advaita).

— TURIYA: THE GOD STATE
Unravel the ancient mystery of Turiya - The God State. The book that demystifies and uncovers the true state of Enlightened beings.

SERENADE OF BLISS SERIES

— SAMADHI: THE FORGOTTEN EDEN
Revealing the Ancient Yogic Art of Samadhi.

— THE YOGIC DHARMA: THE SUPREME YAMAS AND NIYAMAS
A profound, unconventional, & inspiring exposition on the Yogic Dharma principles.

— TANTRA EXPOSED
The Enlightening Path of Tantra. Unveiling the Practical Guide to Eternal Bliss.

All of these books are available @ Amazon as Kindle & Paperback.

Subscribe and receive the ebook **Uncovering the Real** plus updates and information regarding new books or articles, which will be sent about once a month.

www.RealYoga.info

If you have any doubts or questions regarding this or any of the other books, feel free to contact me at:

Santata@RealYoga.info

Special thanks to Eric Robins, who edited and proofread this book with profound love, kindness, and dedication. Your help has been invaluable.

This life is all a dream, a dream within a dream within a dream. We dream this world, we dream that we die and take birth in another body. And in this birth, we dream that we have dreams. All kinds of pleasures and suffering alternate in these dreams, but a moment comes when waking up happens. In this moment, which we call realizing the Self, there is the understanding that all the births, all the deaths, all the sufferings, and all the pleasures were unreal dreams that have finally come to an end.

- Annamalai Swami,
Annamalai Swami Final Talks

TABLE OF CONTENTS

Introduction — 11

The Forgotten Sadhu — 15

Part 1

   1. Paradigm Shift — 17

   2. The Dream Journey Toward Enlightenment — 23

   3. The Illusory Dreamer — 29

   4. The Levels of Lucid Dreaming — 37

Part 2

   5. Awakening the Dreamer — 45

      5.1 Becoming Lucid — 48

      5.2 Questioning The Nature of Dual Reality — 54

      5.3 Dream Journal — 55

      5.4 Enhancing the Chances of Lucidity — 60

      5.5 Consciously Falling Asleep — 67

      5.6 Barely Touching Wakefulness With an Alarm Clock — 74

   6. Stabilizing Awareness — 79

   7. Transforming the Source Code — 87

7.1 The Materialization Practice — 89

7.2 The Mirror Practice — 92

7.3 The Gladiator of the Subconscious Mind — 94

7.4 Interacting with Dream Characters — 97

7.5 The Witness of Dreams — 104

7.6 Enlightening Nightmares — 108

8. Spiritual Practice Within the Dream State — 111

9. Dream Unity and Insights — 117

10. Non-Dual Dream Yoga — 127

10.1 When Dream Lucidity no Longer Matters — 131

11. Liminal Phenomena and Side-Effects — 137

11.1 Sleep Paralysis — 137

11.2 False Awakenings — 139

11.3 Grounding — 142

Part 3

12. The Dream of Wakefulness — 145

12.1 Transcending Bardo — 150

13. The Drop of Water — 153

The Remembered Sadhu — 157

Glossary — 166

Introduction

Lucid dreaming is an ancient art that has been practiced for over two millennia. Since the Ancient Greek philosopher Aristotle first wrote about lucid dreaming, a lot of progress has been made in understanding them.

However, throughout the eons, the essence of lucid dreaming seems to have been forgotten. Instead of being a path toward self-transcendence, lucid dreaming became the goal—and its biggest treasure was lost.

Time and time again, the highest purpose of spirituality becomes overlooked.

As human beings, we always strive for more, and are always looking to transcend our present situation, whatever it may be. But the truth of the matter is that this constant feeling of incompleteness that drives our actions—and the suffering that comes with it—will not go away, not with money, possessions, knowledge, status, or power.

This is where lucid dreaming enters: it gives you the possibility of finding true wholeness and untouchable happiness; it gives you an opportunity for self-transcendence. This is where this book enters.

Most lucid dreaming books fall into one of three categories: scientific, esoteric, or self-development. Although you may find some useful information in these types of books, the first one will be a labyrinth of thoughts and conceptual analysis posing as "genuine knowledge," arousing intellectual satisfaction; the second one will typically be too entangled in old dogmatic traditions and lineages, or filled with rhetoric that reinforces the ego narrative and sense of separation; the third one lacks an enlightenment-oriented non-dual perspective.

This work is not a common lucid dreaming book, but one for those on the path to enlightenment—for those who are on a journey to unveil their original state of being.

All lucid dreaming books teach you how to become lucid in a dream and explore the magnificent dream world. Some more advanced books may even teach you how to use lucidity for psychological progression, shadow work, and self-development. However, the vast majority of them lack one central aspect: understanding lucid dreaming and dream yoga in the context of enlightenment, non-duality, and how to use the dream state to become aware of and transcend the dreamer itself. They all focus on the dream instead of turning back and exploring the dreamer. After all, there's no dream without a dreamer, yet everybody pays attention to the first and ignores the latter.

More than being just a guide to discover lucid dreaming, this book is a guide to discover and transcend *the lucid dreamer*—a guide to Self-discovery and Self-realization.

Wasting too much time and energy in the dream state without utilizing it for a true spiritual purpose is a frequent symptom in many lucid dreamers. But if you're on a journey toward emancipation from suffering and incompleteness, if you're searching for the Reality behind both the waking and dream states, if you're looking for true happiness and inner peace, then you have to pierce through this trap—you have to pierce the veil of Maya and discover what lies ahead.

Every night you are resuscitated from the darkness of sleep by the light of dreams. Will you continue to neglect this other facet of your existence and sleep through them with ignorance, or will you awaken to the infinite potential that the dream state can bring—an awakening into the eternal state of unfathomable bliss? Only you can decide.

The opportunity? It is in your hands, right here, right now.

THE FORGOTTEN SADHU

ॐ

The sun's bright rays gave life to the dim reflection of my face in the water flowing past me. Suddenly, I came back to my senses. I was sitting in what looked like the banks of the Ganga River.

I had completely forgotten. I had just been taught, by a Sadhu, the secret key to unlock the mystery of the Self. The problem? I couldn't remember the teaching.

"What did the Sadhu say?" I asked myself while looking at the river. But I didn't know.

As I kept looking at my reflection, I noticed something strange. It was changing.

"I am dreaming!" I suddenly realized. Eureka.

I looked once again at the reflection and saw it change and

continue changing. This dream river was showing me the flow of life—the constant change in the river of consciousness. From one body to another, from one life to another, from one identity to another, from a story to another, from a face to another, so we flow through the universal river of life. But what are we in the midst of all of these reflections?

At that moment, instead of looking at the transmuting reflection, I looked at what it was made of: water. That reflection was just an illusion; the realness behind it was actually water. Beautiful, moving water. I took a long breath, gazed at the water, and pondered, "What's the realness behind this water?"

I looked at what that water was made of: mental content. This was all my mind—the sun's warm rays, the flowing water, my reflection. I was dreaming, after all.

What if I look at my mind now to see what it's made of?

I woke up.

Part 1

CHAPTER 1
PARADIGM SHIFT

Unlike most lucid dreamers, I don't remember many of the specifics from my first ever lucid dream. In fact, all I can remember is that it happened when I was a child and that in it, I was falling and falling in an unending descent toward an abyss of nothingness. I was fully aware that I was dreaming, yet I couldn't seem to escape that fall. I couldn't fight the dream's gravity—or the void's pull—and I was petrified. I remember waking up startled with my heart racing.

I was also conscious of periods where I was sleeping, yet nothing was occurring. I later discovered that these periods are referred to as deep dreamless sleep—periods where the subject-object dichotomy is no longer present, and thus the individual consciousness is completely unconscious. Yet I remember too that I was blissfully aware.

It took me quite a long time to realize that the lucid dreams I was having were of my individual consciousness being pulled into the nothingness of deep dreamless sleep. I seemed to frequently become conscious when I was on the edge of the dream state, on the verge of duality.

Now, I look back upon those experiences as a blessing because they helped me to see and understand beyond the duality of the dream state, and pointed me toward the very existence of non-dual consciousness (i.e., consciousness with no objects to be conscious of; consciousness only blissfully conscious of itself), though my conscious mind couldn't possibly comprehend such insights at the time.

Many children have had vivid, and perhaps even lucid dreams throughout their childhoods. In adulthood, many people begin to disregard their dreams to the point of not remembering a single dream for weeks or months at a time. Despite this, one thing is still certain: we all dream.

From the time we are infants until we take our very last breath, everybody experiences dreams—it's a universal phenomenon. Everybody knows what a dream is. We've all experienced it.

Whenever we go to sleep, regardless of the time of the day, our physical senses fade into the background, we lose body-awareness, and the world outside shuts down, giving birth to a new, distinct, yet recognizable world. In this dream world, most people are going through it unaware of the nature of their state—they don't know that they're dreaming.

This is where lucid dreaming enters, and it is precisely what the name suggests: being lucid within a dream. In other words, lucid dreaming is a dream where you are aware that you are dreaming; your waking consciousness (i.e., the consciousness with which you experience wakefulness) becomes available to you while you dream.

In lucid dreaming, there's a sense of utter freedom, as if a light suddenly illuminated what once was mere darkness. Those who have their first lucid dream are usually astonished when they realize that they have never truly experienced a dream with such heightened awareness before. It's mind-blowing. Furthermore, since people spend 1/3rd of their lives sleeping, I'd say it's worth exploring dreams and learning how to properly use them on the spiritual path toward enlightenment, especially for spiritual practitioners.

In the physical world, which we access through wakefulness, we have a physical body, an identity, and a personal story. As spiritual practitioners, we can sit down and meditate, perform pranayama, practice Kundalini Yoga, Self-Inquiry, or any number of other spiritual disciplines. Through those spiritual practices, we still and purify our mind, enabling it to probe deeper into its origin.

Although these practices oftentimes intermix with the subconscious mind, they always begin with and are practiced from the waking state. This is understandable because that's where the main issues that people experience occur: the suffering, the lack of happiness, and the feeling of incompleteness. The dream state doesn't feel as bad because, apparently, it ends quickly. It doesn't last, so people don't mind. They may experience suffering in the dream state, just as in the waking state, but they lack the lucidity and discernment that would enable them to become aware of the issue and transcend it. Perhaps if there are recurring nightmares, they may then try to do something about them, such as attending therapy, but usually, since such issues and experiences in the dream state terminate rather swiftly, the majority of people just don't care too much.

However, the dream state is an unpolished gem, and it would be a waste not to use it for authentic spiritual progress. Since the subconscious is the puppeteer and the conscious mind the puppet, if we can get the puppet to control the puppeteer, we may gain freedom from the chains or strings that bind us.

When we're dreaming, we're directly experiencing the

subconscious mind, and thus any mental or psychological effects or changes in the dream state have the potential to manifest in stronger and faster ways than in the waking state—if you manage to achieve a high degree of lucidity and awareness, and use the proper methods. This isn't easy, but if accomplished, it's powerfully efficient.

Dream spiritual practice done right can shorten your path toward Self-Realization and give you wonderful and unimaginable experiences. It's a commitment that shouldn't be taken lightly because it will require a lot of attention, energy, and time. But it's very much worth it.

Gaining waking state consciousness while dreaming enables the opportunity for an astonishing journey of self-discovery. Not only can lucid dreams improve your overall well-being and serve as a platform for self-development, promoting physical and mental health, but they can also become the basis of your spiritual practice that aims at realizing your true nature (or at the very least, aid you in your main sadhana).

Even though lucid dreaming has traditionally been used for personal and egoic reasons, this is not its true goal. The goal of lucid dreaming is to enable the dreamer to also become lucid in the waking state, and then to subsequently transcend both states into non-duality (i.e., into the primordial stateless state of unbroken wholeness). Authentic seekers use lucid dreaming to purify and reprogram their subconscious mind, perform spiritual practice, and realize their true nature.

The taste of the experience of the very moment that you awaken in the dream state is a powerful glimpse that resembles the taste of the freedom of awakening in the waking state. Nobody negates that being awake within a dream seems magnificent, but awakening from what is thought to be a state where you are already awake is the true awakening.

Lucid dreaming leads to *lucid waking*, which then leads to *lucid consciousness*. Lucid consciousness leads to *pure consciousness*. The realization of *pure consciousness* is the crux of lucid dreaming.

CHAPTER 2

THE DREAM JOURNEY TOWARD ENLIGHTENMENT

Each night, or whenever you fall asleep, you enter into the wondrous world of dreams. Even if you don't recall dreaming when you wake up, that doesn't mean you didn't dream—it just means you don't remember your dreams[1]. Everybody dreams when they disconnect from their physical vehicle.

A dream is also very similar to the waking state, in the sense that you experience a world, memories, goals, likes, dislikes, feelings, thoughts, emotions, sensations, and so on (that you believe are yours). You have a "dream" personality, a "dream" identity, and a "dream" story. You can even wake up inside of the dream, live your dream "daily life," and at

---

[1] Believing that one doesn't dream is akin to believing one doesn't breathe just because one isn't aware of the breathing. Pointing you toward the breath will make you aware of it, just like pointing you to dreams and lucidity will make you aware of them.

night (in the dream), you go to "sleep." Although there are some apparent differences, the dream and the waking state are quite similar. There are inconsistencies in the dream state that you may deem impossible in the waking state, but these are only noticed upon waking up. When you are dreaming, everything seems perfectly fine to you—it is only after waking up that you recognize how impossible and illogical some parts of the dream actually were.

However, if you dive deeper into the relationship between the dreamer and the dream, you will realize that when you are in the dream state, most of the time you aren't really a "dreamer"—you are just an oblivious individual living in a world that you consider real, just like in the waking state. You are unaware of the dream's illusory nature while in it, confined to an illusionary prison surrounded not by iron bars, but by bars made of deceptive and mistaken impressions.

If you are not aware that you are dreaming, you are experiencing what you think is reality, and therefore you are not a dreamer in the same sense that you are not a dreamer in the physical reality either. You only become a dreamer under two circumstances: the first scenario, which is the most common, occurs once you wake up in the physical reality and experience the memories of the dream. There, you remember your dream and know that you were a dreamer.

The second scenario represents a different kind of dreamer—a lucid dreamer—where you awaken and realize that the nature of the reality you are in is but an illusion, and therefore you are able to transcend its deceptive walls and contents, because you know your mind created them. Where once you thought you were a mere content or figment of the whole, you now realize that you are both the individual content *and* the whole. Such insight allows you to effortlessly cross through the illusory prison bars that previously seemed impassable, and fly ahead into the vast world of the mind. You are a lucid dreamer right there.

However, you are still bound by your mind—the large majority of it escaping your conscious control—and its created universe. To be free from all constraints, regardless of how subtly they may manifest, you have to go back to the origin of the dream universe, before there was even a subject-object dichotomy. And since the mind is the creator of the dream universe, you have to go into its innermost core to discover the ultimate freedom; you have to go beyond being a "dreamer," regardless of whether it's a lucid or nonlucid one—you have to be the unmanifested Reality itself.

But before all of this is even possible, it starts with becoming lucid in a dream, something common sense may dictate is impossible to accomplish. That being said, if you're reading this book, I'm confident that you have expanded way beyond traditional acumen at this point. In fact, lucid dreaming is not only possible, but you will actually learn how to achieve it in this book.

If you've already had an experience or glimpse of becoming lucid in a dream, you undeniably know how mesmerizing it feels. The experience of being lucid is not merely an interesting experience or state—it infuses you with life, energy, creativity, intelligence, vitality, and sometimes, an indomitable will to explore and transcend your inner world.

Lucid dreaming can be practiced for many virtuous purposes such as expanding the spectrum of perception and experience from the ordinary gross senses to the subtle inner senses, or as a form of embarking on the challenge of unearthing a purpose for your life that's currently buried deep in your subconscious, or even as a tool for self-development.

Nevertheless, its highest purpose is the realization of our blissful and deathless nature, also known as spiritual enlightenment or Self-Realization.

To achieve this, there is a specific system of progression that must be followed, and it is divided into six general steps:

1. Becoming lucid;
2. Stabilizing lucidity;
3. Purifying and reprogramming the subconscious mind;
4. Performing meditation and spiritual practice within the dream;
5. Surrendering both the dream and the dreamer;
6. Practicing non-dual Dream Yoga.

Becoming aware within the dream is just the first part, and perhaps the most straightforward. After being lucid, we have to stabilize lucidity, which may pose some difficulties due to the volatile nature of the dream state. The dream state is very volatile, but it's also exceptional for spiritual practice because we are actively within the subconscious, where everything we do is "on steroids"— all effects are stronger and easier to achieve, but paradoxically, also harder to sustain and make permanent.

Once we have attained consistent lucidity, we can progress into purifying our subconscious mind, its unconscious tendencies, and our karmic seeds. This is all done through interacting with, exploring, understanding, and transcending our subconscious manifestations and contents within the dream state, which is very different from sitting spiritual practice that is done in the waking state.

Only after enough subconscious debris have been cleared, can we proceed to some of the more commonly understood "spiritual practices;" however, instead of performing them in the waking state, they will be done in the dream state. They will feel different when compared to practicing them in the waking state, but the premise is the same, and some similarities will inevitably emerge.

Eventually, this process culminates in the relinquishing and subsequent eradication of the dream and dream-ego, transcending beyond the veil of the dream state into immaculate non-dual consciousness.

Throughout this process, the dreamer not only becomes lucid to the fact that they are dreaming, but also becomes aware that their own lucidity is still another level of dreaming. Transcending lucidity of dreams into lucidity of consciousness itself, regardless of its current state (wakefulness or dreaming), is the lucidity of the gods. That's our destination.

CHAPTER 3

THE ILLUSORY DREAMER

The biggest obstacle in using lucid dreams to "attain" enlightenment is not in actually becoming lucid, stabilizing lucidity, remembering your spiritual goal, or in performing spiritual practice within the dream. The biggest obstacle is the lack of understanding and discernment concerning the nature of the dreamer.

Despite the usefulness of lucid dreaming, it occurs in the domain of the ego, and thus, just like in meditation, Kriya Yoga, or in most spiritual practices, this is its playground unless approached with a non-dual purpose.

Every spiritual seeker must understand that:

It is the ego that dreams.

It is the ego that becomes lucid.

It is the ego that experiences lucid dreaming and then wakes up again into the waking state.

Lucid dreaming is but a play of the "I-ego"—different setting but the same old story. This knowledge is tremendously critical, and though it is not something the vast majority of lucid dreaming literature will tell you, it must be known prior to practicing lucid dreaming for enlightenment purposes, otherwise lucid dreaming practice will most likely trap the seeker in a maze of experiences, states, and fireworks.

However, just because lucid dreaming is within the ego's realm, that doesn't mean we can't use it to transcend the ego.

Lucid dreaming that is merely used to explore the dream world, fulfill desires and fantasies, improve psychological conditioning, purify blockages, or even for standard spiritual practice, won't take you all the way—it will remain within the ego's dimension. After all, it is the ego that dreams, explores, fulfills desires, improves or worsens its psychological conditioning, purifies blockages, or meditates. But lucid dreaming that uses the aforementioned as a starting off point for non-dual dream practice—that's definitely not a play of the ego.

But who is the lucid dreamer, and what is this ego or "I-ego"?

> "Ego is "I," the thought "I." Before anything can be, such as "I am a man" or "I am a woman," "I" has to be there. "I" is, therefore, the foundation of duality. All

duality stands on "I." Without "I," there can never be a "you," an "other," or anything else.

There are different types of definitions of what ego means, but in this book, ego means the thought "I," which is based on the belief "I am the body." All conditionings, which pertain to the psychological mind are based on the notion of "I," or "I am the body."

The ego can have millions of adjuncts (...). Changing all of those adjuncts (e.g., an aggressive person undergoes therapy and comes out calm and kind), does not change the ego ("I"). It only changes its adjuncts. An "I" is always an "I" unless it is dissolved (enlightenment).

Robert was born a male: "I am Robert" - "I am a man." When he was 21 years old, he underwent male-to-female gender reassignment surgery, becoming "Jessie," a woman: "I am Jessie" - "I am a woman."

Did the "I" change?

No. The underlying principle of being an individual self remained, even though two core adjuncts changed—the name and gender."

- THE YOGA OF CONSCIOUSNESS

It is evident that all dreams require a dreamer, including lucid dreams—there has to be an individuality ("I-ego") who is within the dream and aware of the fact that they are dreaming.

However, non-lucid dreams are quite different from lucid dreams. Most of the time, they are manifestations of the subconscious processing and organization of information and knowledge regarding what happened or is currently happening in your life. There are countless examples of how our dreams are inundated with our current waking life issues. For example:

Susan is having some family complications. Her mother doesn't like Susan's fiancé, and told her she would not attend their wedding. It seems like Susan has to choose between her husband-to-be and her mother, and it's causing her a lot of stress. When she goes to sleep at night, she dreams that she is in a small room with two transparent doors. One door leads to her parent's house, a familiar, cozy place; the second door leads to an unknown location because all Susan can see is the sky. She initially moves toward the first door but then looks back at the second and an immense feeling of freedom emerges. Based on this, she decides to pass through the second door and jump into the sky. As soon as she does this, she starts to fall precipitously, gets scared, and begins pondering whether she made the right choice. As she's falling, though, an ecstatic feeling of freedom materializes in her heart, and she starts flying. Then she wakes up.

This dream is reflecting Susan's internal turmoil and her subconscious decision. Although this was an explicit dream (i.e., its meaning was obvious), she might have experienced any one of a number of diverse ways through which her subconscious manifested her internal conflicts.

Here's a different situation:

Niels is a physicist, and he wants to discover and understand the atomic structure of the atom. He's constantly contemplating and thinking about this subject, but can't seem to arrive at any solid insights.

One night he goes to sleep, and because he's been so emotionally, intellectually, and mentally involved with this subject, his subconscious visually manifests the solution in his dream, enabling him to discover that the atom has electrons that go around a nucleus, similar to planets orbiting the Sun.

This dream reflected Neil's internal struggle to find a solution.

All of the insights that you may experience in a typical non-lucid dream are aimed at solving problems that won't truly advance you toward Self-realization. Lucidity is crucial for this.

With lucidity, the dream-ego/dream-self becomes the waking-ego/waking-self, though this always depends on the degree of lucidity. With a low degree of lucidity, the dream-ego has conscious access to some of the memories, ideas, and views of the waking-ego; it typically carries the waking-ego's conditioning and patterns because they both share the same subconscious source, even though many of its "facets" and dispositions may be dissimilar to its waking version.

As the degree of lucidity increases, the more resemblances it has to the waking-ego. In full-blown lucidity, the dream-ego becomes the waking-ego.

When you don't remember a dream, that's because it was a different "identity" of your "I" experiencing that dream; same "I," different identities. Hence the memory of the dream-ego gets buried into the subconscious and there's no remembrance of it in the waking state. When you wake up from a non-lucid dream, you have a small window of opportunity to remember your dream because, at that moment, both identities are slightly "intermixed."

It is imperative to understand that the "I-ego" is never

asleep while dreaming; it is your identity attached to the "I," your story, likes, dislikes, ideas, and characteristics of your current waking-self or waking-ego—the one reading these words—that is asleep. Being lucid in a dream simply means that the waking-ego has merged with the dream-ego, regardless of whether this is accomplished either partially or fully.

In lucid dreaming that is practiced to "achieve" enlightenment, we want to unify both egos, creating a strong bridge between waking and dreaming, and being fully conscious of this process.

When, through spiritual practice, a connection is made between the subconscious mind and the conscious mind in the waking state, achieving lucidity becomes an easier and smoother process. That's one of the reasons why, for lucid dreaming, prior meditative experience is extremely useful. By infusing waking state consciousness into the dream state subconsciousness during waking state practices, we more easily remember our purpose of becoming Self-Realized during dreams, and can successfully use the dream state to achieve it.

In lucid dreaming, understanding the role of the "I-ego" is key. You should neither shun it nor repress your dream individuality. It may seem that you are unable to control the dream-ego from the waking state, but by first becoming lucid and then by using it to fulfill your purpose of self-liberation, you can free yourself from the illusory walls that perpetuate your egoic and limited existence. The dream-ego can then fulfill its ultimate purpose of being a vehicle toward self-transcendence. This is the way of the lucid dreamer.

CHAPTER 4

THE LEVELS OF LUCID DREAMING

Common dreams typically fall under two categories:

- Dreams about daily residual impressions, unresolved concerns or preoccupations;

- Dreams about buried emotional recollections from any period of our lives (i.e., dreams with karmic residues, deep emotional shadows, or latent tendencies).

The first is the most common type of dream, while the latter, in addition to also being commonplace, may repeat during different periods of our lives, even though such buried recollections may manifest differently from dream to dream.

In both of these instances, our subconscious mind is trying to process, organize, restructure, and understand these impressions, emotions, recollections, and matters.

In rare instances, dreams may be about previous lifetimes; we are being shown something relevant, regardless of whether it is a positive or negative *samskara* (i.e., previous mental impressions and recollections). These dreams mostly occur when someone is non-lucid, though one could easily gain lucidity in them through practice.

Then, there's a completely different type of dream altogether—we'll call them *spiritual dreams*. While these types of dreams may occur to anyone, they're more likely to happen to those who assiduously do waking state spiritual practice and perform lucid dreaming for spiritual purposes. They are dreams that have profound spiritual significance and can function as breakthrough moments in our spiritual journey.

The more we practice lucid dreaming and use it as a vehicle for spiritual advancement, the more our ordinary dreams (those containing superficial impressions) diminish, creating space for more spirituality-oriented dreams. This is a cycle that gets more powerful with each iteration; as there are less debris and confusion in our subconscious each time, the mind requires less time to "clean" them, allowing us to go directly to where it's most important.

Lucid dreaming practice can be used for a myriad of personal or spiritual objectives. Each objective differs according to the seeker's spiritual maturity, and depending on your level, lucid dreaming may have a different purpose. Here I will divide the usefulness of lucid dreaming into different levels:

(Level 1)

At this initial level, lucid dreaming serves the purpose of showing you that it is indeed possible to be awake while dreaming, and that the dream state is as real to the senses as the waking state. This will expand your mind's horizons of what's possible, providing one of many out-of-the-box paradigm shifts. Oftentimes, the senses will be enhanced, and you may experience more vivid perceptions.

(Level 2)

After realizing that lucid dreaming is a possibility, the *oneironaut* can use it to experience impossible things (e.g., flying or going through a wall), to test the physics and limits of what's possible in the dream state, and to break the conventional "handicaps" that are typically carried over from the waking state. For example, there's no gravity in the dream state; yet you will experience it out of habit brought from the waking state. Many first-time lucid dreamers cannot successfully fly because of this—and due to the ingrained notion that humans taking off and flying like a bird is not possible—they can only jump higher. These limitations from the waking state have to be broken because they don't exist in the dream state.

At this level, the oneironaut can also use lucid dreaming to fulfill personal desires (e.g., climbing Mount Everest or driving a *Bugatti Chiron*), either for fun and pleasure, or as an attempt to extinguish karmic seeds. Depending on your grade of lucidity, these experiences in the dream state can be felt exactly as they'd be in the waking state (sometimes even more vividly).

Fulfilling desires in the dream state may quench one's thirst for those achievements in the waking state, but it can also rebound and make you want to physically experience them even more. As you extinguish the seed of a desire by tasting its fruit, you can begin acquiring a taste for more of these types of fruits. There's nothing wrong with that, but it will be counterproductive if your real goal is enlightenment.

If you understand that what you ultimately want is to be happy, and that the only reason you want to fulfill a specific desire is because you believe the achievement of that thing will bring you happiness, then you will not desire it anymore; instead, you will only wish for perfect happiness, perfect bliss, perfect peace, and perfect ecstasy. And do you know what can give you that? The realization of your true unbounded blissful nature. That is finding God.

(Level 3)

At this point, lucid dreaming is useful to help the seeker achieve different insights and realizations concerning the origin, experience, and end of the dream state and to see how that also applies to the waking state. There are more parallels than differences to be found.

Through these small yet important realizations, a stronger bridge is built between the waking-self and the dreaming-self.

(Level 4)

This is where things get interesting, and also where the main spiritual practices in this book begin. You are now directly conscious that you are accessing, engaging, and working with the subconscious mind, as well as, in some instances, connecting with the collective field of consciousness of humankind. Through specific practices, you can purify your mind and reprogram your subconscious to be more prone to higher forms of spiritual practice and enlightenment. In addition to extinguishing the seeds that give rise to desires, you also realize that the orchard doesn't belong to you.

This process will often involve interaction with anthropomorphized conscious and unconscious aspects of your mind, whose purpose is to help you relate and translate the information better, and to propel you toward a more in-depth process of self-discovery and realization.

(Level 5)

Once you have achieved a higher degree of discernment and your mind is at the required level of maturity, spiritual practice and meditation that have been performed in the waking state can also be performed in the dream state with great results. There will be some differences between "waking state sadhana" and "dream state sadhana," but their general framework and purpose will be the same. In other words, Yoga can now be practiced in the dream state, which may produce stronger effects than in the waking state, as long as it's done properly. Lucid dreaming now becomes Dream Yoga[2].

Since the waking consciousness is operating from the vast

---

[2] Typically, lucid dreaming is different from Dream Yoga in the sense that unlike the first, the latter is used as a means toward enlightenment.

subconscious realm of instant manifestation, spiritual practices performed within the dream state have the potential to be much more powerful, though that may come with higher volatility. If properly done, this more immediate effect of practice can boost progress and create the required stillness in the mind to allow it to look back at itself in its true form of objectless consciousness, even within the unstable nature of the dream state.

(Level 6)

In this last level, we use our heightened lucidity within the dream state to look back at our core, thus becoming aware of the dreamer, of "I," of the ego's kernel. After purifying the blocking facets of the "I-ego," we pierce its bullseye and abide in its center of contentless consciousness.

At this point, whichever state we are in—waking, dreaming, or deep dreamless sleep—is irrelevant. We go all the way to our non-dual source of being and abide there. This is the ultimate level of lucid dreaming.

Part 2

CHAPTER 5

AWAKENING THE DREAMER

Becoming lucid within a dream is the first step in lucid dreaming; it's also the most important, because without lucidity, nothing is achieved.

Most books about lucid dreaming succeed in giving wonderful methods to achieve it; however, there are so many books and methods available that readers may be overwhelmed when first encountering this subject. As always, I prefer to go for simplicity and straightforwardness, and that's why we will limit the methods to those that work the best according to my direct experience. If you prefer, you can practice any alternative method as long as it enables you to achieve lucidity within a dream[3].

---

[3] Lucid dreaming can be a spontaneous occurrence for those who are diligent with their waking sadhanas when such practices involve deep consciousness work.

"Becoming lucid" may itself be an ambiguous term because there are different grades of lucidity within a dream:

1) Slight Lucidity

You have a fuzzy awareness that you are dreaming. You can make some decisions semi-consciously, but you're still very much subject to the events and contents of the dream. You can easily slip out of lucidity into non-lucidity; it's slightly easier to remember dreams once you wake up (and this is vastly improved by using a dream journal).

2) Lucidity

You are completely aware that you are dreaming. You make all decisions consciously, but you're still not in control of what happens within the dream; in other words, you're still subject to the events and happenings within the dream. You cannot shape the dream into a productive practice for enlightenment because you lack the whole-being awareness that everything in the dream is actually your mind. You have no real authority in the dream, and you probably can't go through walls, fly, or perform supernatural feats easily. You may still lose partial or full lucidity.

3) Full Lucidity

You are truly lucid within the dream, and you can mold it. You're able to perform any supernatural feats. You're capable of "summoning" archetypes or personal subconscious traits by anthropomorphizing them for an easier interaction. You can consciously interact with dream characters, perform spiritual practice, and navigate through your mind's dream world. You seldom lose lucidity. Reprogramming the subconscious and purifying the mind become possible. You can subject yourself to the trials of the dream-world spiritual path.

4) Transpersonal Lucidity

Your lucid awareness lies at the end of the spectrum. Everything is felt as a unison of consciousness. There's awareness of separation within the dream state in order to facilitate perception and self-observance, but there's a continuity of the knowingness of oneness. "Everything in the dream is I" (your mind) is not a concept or abstraction, but is rather your living knowledge.

5) Beyond Lucidity

Perception (providing the experience of somethingness and separation), and lack-of-perception (providing the experience of nothingness) both unify into pure consciousness. The dream, dreamer, and the experience of dreaming collapse into their one source: consciousness, God, or the true Self.

In this chapter, we're only concerned about achieving grades 1 and 2 of lucidity. The next chapter is where you can learn how to stabilize your lucidity and establish grade 2 as the baseline, so that you can then jump into grade 3, which is where spiritual practices can be successfully done. As you continue practicing, you will naturally progress from grade 1 up to grade 4 of lucidity. Grade 5 falls within the realm of non-dual Dream Yoga.

Becoming Lucid

You can learn how to become lucid within a dream. To do so, you must develop a keen interest in dreams and cultivate a strong desire and intention for becoming lucid. Additionally, there are three main requirements:

- Performing present moment state and reality checks throughout the day to question the reality of where you are (awake or dreaming);

- Being capable of bridging waking consciousness into

dreaming subconsciousness by expanding the threshold on which you are conscious.

- Having a dream journal to improve dream recollection.

Lucid dreaming can be initiated from either the dreaming or the waking state. The first occurs when you are dreaming and then you become lucid (nonlucid dreaming consciousness -> lucid dreaming consciousness); the latter occurs from the waking state when you are lucid and then you consciously enter into a dream (waking consciousness -> lucid dreaming consciousness).

The first form is typically the most common and accessible—you are dreaming and gradually or suddenly realize it. This is achieved when you notice a discrepancy, inconsistency, or something bizarre within the dream, and doubt whether that can be "real." This brief moment of suspicion leads you to perform a check on the nature of your current reality and state, and if successful, you realize that you must be in a dream. Such strange circumstances or events occur all the time in the dream state, but they are often overlooked and unrecognized for what they are.

Depending upon the degree of your self-awareness and clarity with which you test your current state and reality, you will achieve a differing grade of lucidity. The effect that results from the birth of lucidity is equivalent to the degree of purity and maturity of the dreamer's mind.

Most of the time, when something that makes no sense whatsoever occurs within the dream state, we don't question it, and even if we do, our minds rationalize it and convince us that somehow, such bizarre occurrences or things make sense. However, it is precisely when we realize that something is offbeat that we should inquire whether we are dreaming, and then proceed to perform a "reality check" to know whether we are in the dream state or not. The realness of perception is not a valid indicator of the dream state because dreams really do look real (and sometimes even more so than the waking state). The vividness of "reality" is not the barometer of the state we are in. In fact, dreams look so utterly real that they systematically delude you into accepting their reality unconditionally, night after night.

The trick to imprinting the awareness of checking your state in the dream world is to perform it in the waking world as well. In other words, you need to practice reality checks while awake whenever something strange, unexpected, or bizarre happens. Basically, you will train your mind to question its current state whenever something out of the ordinary occurs, or when you're in any emotionally engrossing circumstance. By conditioning it to do so, whenever something offbeat happens in the dream state, you will automatically question your reality and perform the check, injecting the waking state lucidity into the dream if you confirm that you are dreaming.

It's imperative to perform reality checks even on the smallest of suspicions because otherwise, it will always look like "this is real; can't be a dream," and you won't become lucid.

In my view, the single best and most reliable test to know whether you are dreaming or not is to perform the *breath-check*:

Try to breathe while your fingers *firmly* seal your nose. Try it multiple times. If it doesn't work, you are not dreaming; if you breathe while your nose is sealed, then you are dreaming. This must be performed throughout the day, just as aforementioned.

To go one step further, after trying the breath-check, look at your hands and check whether they appear normal. Close and open them, and look at the palms and backs of the hands. If the hands are missing a finger (or have an extra one), are deformed in any way, or there's something abnormal with them, you are dreaming. This is called the *hands-check*. I suggest that you always perform these two checks back to back. If you are dreaming, both will fail.

To recapitulate, this is what you are supposed to do:

During the day, whenever something strange, unexpected, or bizarre happens, stop for a moment and bring your awareness to the present moment. Ask yourself: "Am I dreaming?" Perform the breath-check, followed by the hand-check. If both of these two tests fail—i.e., you can breathe with your nose sealed and your hands don't look normal—you are not in the waking state but are dreaming. Once you realize you are dreaming, your awareness and energy levels will skyrocket, and you will become even more lucid.

These two tests have always worked for me. They'll work for you too, as long as they are done with proper attention and awareness. I've tried many other checks, and none of them worked 100% of the time. Whenever you perform them during the daytime, use your utmost attention, so that when you perform them while dreaming, you will use the same focus and attention. Inadequate reality testing will prevent you from becoming lucid because your mind will rationalize whatever it is that is a sign that you're dreaming.

There are many other ways to find out whether you are dreaming or not, such as experiencing recurrent dreams, recognizing familiar dream locations, characters, and signs, or by directly perceiving the unstable nature of the dream.

Examples of the latter are trying to read text and seeing if it is readable; if it changes when you look away and then try to reread it, then you are dreaming; or looking at a mirror and seeing if the reflection changes. However, these tests depend on the conditions of the dream (e.g., there has to be something specific near you that you can use as a reality test, such as the reading example), while the breath-check and hand-check do not require the presence of any "external" conditions.

Fundamentally, if you never question whether you are dreaming during the waking state, you will never do it while dreaming either. You must infuse your subconscious with a desire for and focus on this inquiry. As you progress on your spiritual path and lucid dreaming practice, you will become lucid much faster without needing to thoroughly self-examine your state; just by seeing inconsistences, you will get a feel for knowing right away as to whether you are dreaming or not; or there may be a spontaneous realization of the subtle dream-like attributes, structure, and nature of the current experience that let you know you are dreaming. Nonetheless, I still advise you to reality-check your state afterward in these cases, just to make sure.

QUESTIONING THE NATURE OF DUAL REALITY

Performing reality checks in the waking state may seem absurd since you know for sure that you aren't dreaming, right? It's silly—or is it?

Always remember this principle: whatever happens in the waking state, whatever you feel in the waking state, whatever emotion you experience in the waking state, whatever you perceive in the waking state, or whatever you think about in the waking state—you can do all these in the dream state.

If it seems foolish to do reality checks in the waking state because you're so confident that you're not dreaming, it will seem foolish in the dream state as well. Conducting checks on the reality of your state throughout the day is critical and must not be overlooked. Acquiring this habit during wakefulness will carry over into the dream state and propel you to become lucid.

Stop for a moment, feel yourself present right now. Ask yourself, "Am I dreaming?"

Now, breathe in and breathe out. Be aware. Perform the breath-check and hands-check. Blink your eyes twice. Reread this paragraph and see if the text is still the same.

If none of the tests failed, then you aren't dreaming. Do you see how this test may quickly become silly to your mind? There may come a time when before performing the check, you will think, "Why am I doing this, I know for sure that I am not dreaming." You may even wonder how you are going to perform it every day, but once you have your first lucid dream, thanks to a failed reality check done within the dream state, it will confirm that your continuous efforts were worth it. It doesn't matter if you are in the waking or dreaming state—you should approach both states in the same way when it comes to stopping what you're doing and testing the nature of reality.

This doesn't mean that you have to become obsessive and acquire a mentality or behavior of always being doubtful regarding the reality of the state you're in all the time. You must harmonize reality checking with life, and as long as you don't perform it mechanically, over time, it will be smoother and become second nature.

Dream Journal

Imagine that you were chosen to participate in the first human-crewed space mission toward Saturn's moon Titan, using a special futuristic spaceship that can travel quite fast.

You'd set off from Earth to explore Titan and then come back, all within a year. Would you keep a log of your journey?

Of course you would. You'd record everything you see, experience, feel, etc., and not just for the scientists and researchers back on Earth, but also for yourself. You'd need to have a journal that catalogs and details all that you've experienced and perceived, otherwise so much could happen that you might forget some parts later on.

In fact, throughout history, all great explorers have kept a journal, log, or diary of their journey and adventures. Lucid dreaming is no different. Having a dream journal is a critical component of achieving lucidity in dreams. It helps to bring the subconscious and conscious worlds together, significantly improves dream recall, helps to identify dream signals, and so on. Always keep it next to your bed.

Our dream memories must be written in that journal as best as we can recall them. I've used three different methods with great success:

a) Writing them with a pen on a paper;

b) Writing them digitally on a smartphone or a similar device;

c) Recording them with your own voice.

There are differences between these three methods, and you can try each to discover which one you prefer. *a)* is the most traditional one, and it works great as long as you can read what you wrote afterward, as sometimes you may be sleepy, and your handwriting may not be the most legible.

Since most people have a smartphone by their bed these days, journaling your dreams on one might also be a solution, as long as the screen luminosity doesn't startle you and ruin the rest of your night. There are some lucid dreaming applications that may help you keep an organized log, etc. This is *b)*, and it has the great benefit of allowing you to use the "search" function to search for keywords or specific dreams amongst hundreds or thousands of dream logs.

c) You can also use a voice recorder, or a device like a smartphone to record your dream log. This may be the fastest method of recording your dreams but is my least favorite of the three because you can't quickly read or search for dreams and keywords unless you write them down afterward, or use voice-to-text software.

After waking up from the dream, write/record it down as quickly as possible while it's still fresh in your memory. If you don't remember much, start by writing down keywords, and more dream memories will begin to emerge. If you don't remember anything at all, it's okay. Make an effort to remember anything, even just a little detail, and write it down. Things will get progressively better.

Dreams *must* be written down right after you open your physical eyes. If you wait more than a couple of minutes, you will forget about half of the dream; if you wait more than 10 minutes, the dream will be mostly lost. Be quick.

After writing down the keywords and details about the dream, give it a title that exemplifies what the dream is about. If it's your first dream, write #1 somewhere there; if it's the second, write #2, and so on (never repeat the same number). Once everything is done, register the present hour and minutes. Do this for all recorded dreams.

If it's a lucid dream, write *LUCID DREAM* before or after the title, or somewhere easily identifiable for later check. In the dream description, make sure you mention what triggered lucidity, and why and when the dream ended.

If you're voice recording a dream, you can execute the same instructions, and save the file with the dream title. Make sure the date and hour are also automatically saved. It won't be as smooth as writing them down.

It doesn't matter if you recall almost nothing when you wake up—as long as you keep recording little things here and there, your "dream memory" will improve, and soon enough you'll be scribbling down multiple dreams per night. This is how you begin to show your mind that dream recall is important.

As you keep writing down your dreams, you'll detect that there are recurring symbols, signs, dream characters, circumstances, or events in your dreams. If you study your dream journal and imbue these repeating patterns into your mind, you will be able to use them as lucidity-triggers. In other words, once you see that same sign or dream character, or experience the same event, you will inquire whether you are dreaming, perform the subsequent reality checks, and become lucid. Considering that these are symbols or things that you experience repeatedly, it's very probable that you will become lucid as soon as you see or experience one.

At the end of the day, the purpose of a dream journal is not to write down the murky recollections of a nightly slumber, but to depict the tale of your inner adventures. If you're serious about lucid dreaming, you will have one.

Enhancing the Chances of Lucidity

Lucid dreams will most often be initiated from the dream state when, while you are in a dream, you realize that you are dreaming. However, to enhance even more your chances of becoming lucid, you should not attempt to practice lucid dreaming when you go to sleep at night.

Typically, as you lay in your bed ready to fall asleep, you (with waking consciousness) begin to feel your mind scattering into thoughts and dream imagery. Soon enough, hypnagogic hallucinations[4] of all forms take the better of your wakefulness, and you doze off, transitioning into light sleep, and eventually, you'll fall asleep and enter into deep sleep.

You should never attempt to practice lucid dreaming in this initial phase of sleep; your body and mind need to rest, and the REM sleep phase where dreams occur is nonexistent or very short-lived at the beginning of the sleep cycle.

As the night goes on, you naturally go through various sleep cycles consisting of deep sleep, light sleep, and REM. In the beginning, the deep sleep periods will be long, while REM

---

[4] Hypnagogia is the experience of the transitional state between the waking state and sleep. This wakefulness-sleep transition is teeming with mental phenomena of all kinds.

will be short. Eventually, as the night progresses, the deep sleep cycles become shorter, while the REM periods become longer. Since dreams mostly occur during the REM stage, and the last couple of REM cycles (in the early morning hours) are the longest and the ones where you're the most mentally and physically rested (because you've already gone through most deep sleep phases), they are the best stage for lucid dreaming practice. However, the issue is that after several sleep cycles, your intention to become lucid in a dream will probably no longer be present in your mind with enough strength to inundate your dreams[5].

To counter this, there's a trick we can use to take advantage of these late REM stages, which is to interrupt our sleep cycle in its latter stages by waking up early, waiting for 15 to 20 minutes, and then going back to bed with full intention and resolution to become lucid. This method is commonly called *Wake Back To Bed*.

It is very simple: set your alarm clock to go off 2 to 3 hours earlier than normal. For example, if you go to sleep at midnight intending to wake up at 8 AM, you must set your alarm clock at 5 or 6 AM. If you sleep for 7 hours, set your alarm at 4 to 5 hours after going to sleep.

---

[5] Of course, the more engrossed you get into lucid dreaming, the higher the chances of remembering your goal of becoming lucid. Reading this book will help with that.

By doing this, you are bringing your consciousness back to wakefulness for 15 to 20 minutes, and then going back to sleep to catch the most useful REM period[6].

Let's suppose you go to sleep at 10:30 PM and that you sleep for 7 ½ hours. Here's an example of how to do it[7]:

1. Perform reality checks throughout the day whenever a bizarre or strange event occurs. Have a dream journal to help identify dream signs and to improve the connection between waking and dreaming consciousness. Read something connected to lucid dreaming, such as this book.

2. Set the alarm clock at 4 AM (5 ½ hours of sleep). Go to sleep at 10:30 PM with the steadfast resolution to become lucid.

3. Wake up at 4 AM. Immediately perform the breath-check to see if you are really awake. You will be groggy. If you confirm that you are in the waking state, try to remember some dreams you might've had during the night, and write them

---

[6] If you have a hard time falling asleep after getting up and going back to bed, instead of 2 to 3 hours, you may need to put your alarm clock 3 ½ to 4 hours earlier than you usually would. This depends very much on each practitioner, so you must try and see how much time works best for you.

[7] Late afternoon naps also work in a similar way to this method, as long as you feel that you're able to fall asleep. A 30 to 45 minute nap may enable you to have a lucid dream.

down in your dream journal. Then, stand up and go to the bathroom to wash your face and drink some water. Afterward, sit somewhere comfortable and reflect on what you want—to become lucid in a dream. You can read this book to help flood your mind with the idea and motivation of becoming lucid, or do some spiritual practice or meditation. If you begin to fall asleep when doing some form of spiritual practice, don't do it. Just do something that keeps you awake that is related to lucid dreaming or spirituality; you can read your dream journal, or perform multiple reality checks (breath-check, hand-check, mirror-check, reading-check, etc.). Do not perform physical exercise or anything similar. Keep your body relaxed.

4. Go back to bed at 4:20 AM (give or take). Have the firm intention that you will realize that you're dreaming in your next dream. You can lay down on your back (it may help with lucidity), but if you can't fall asleep on your back, any position is fine.

5. Now there are two ways you can perform this step:

5a. As you lay in bed falling asleep, keep reminding yourself that you will be aware that you are dreaming in your next dream. Let go, and eventually, a dream will come and something may trigger your lucidity.

5b. As you lay down in bed, stay in the supine position and ride the hypnagogic state.

While drifting in and out of sleep, choose something non-physical to place your attention on: a chakra, a visualization, etc. Let's go with the Third-Eye, for example.

Focus on the Third-Eye, the point between your eyebrows, for about 30 seconds—then let it go for 5 seconds. This creates a mental anchor in the conscious mind, and even though awareness is going deeper within, unconsciousness will not take hold of you. This can be called *mental anchoring*.

You must keep the focus on your anchor while intermittently allowing your mind to let go and drift into the borderline of sleep. In the letting-go moments, you can even allow yourself to let go of trying to become lucid, and engage in all sorts of unintelligible thoughts and imagery as you typically do before falling asleep.

This should be done for shorter and shorter periods of concentration, always increasing the "letting go" time. Start with 30 seconds of Third-Eye focus, and 5 seconds of letting go; then after a few rounds like this, 25 seconds of Third-Eye focus, and 10 seconds of letting your mind wander; keep doing this method until you reach 5 seconds of focusing on the Third-Eye, and 30 seconds of letting go. You don't have to count the exact number of seconds; use an approximate estimate and do it by feeling.

As you perform this method of drifting on the borderline of sleep, you will observe hypnagogic phenomena including indistinct forms and shades, senses of movement, or muddled thought-patterns, and you may even suddenly find yourself within a dream at any time.

The repetitive motion of "paying attention to something" and "letting go of all attention into nothing" creates an interesting phenomenon: you are gaining consciousness after letting it go, conditioning your mind to gain lucidity within unconsciousness.

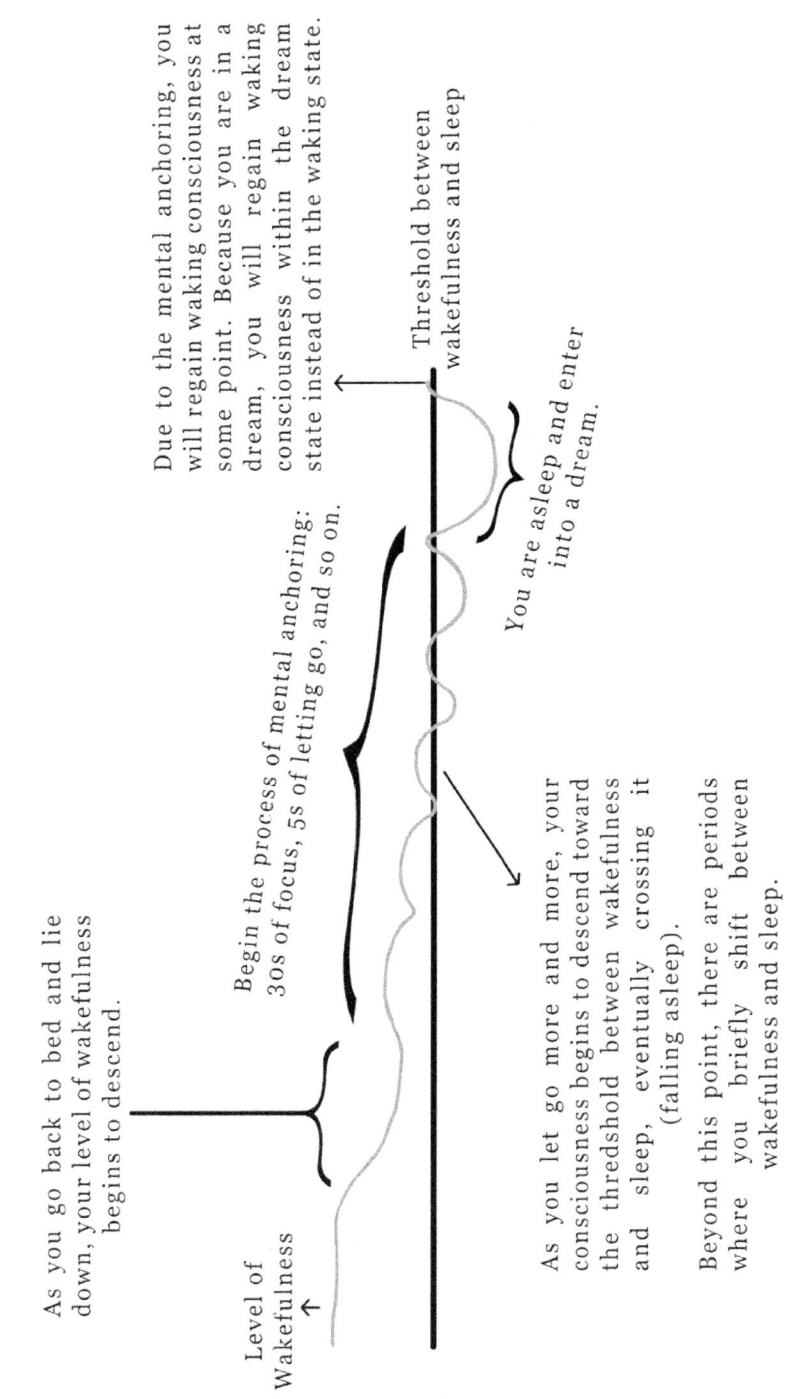

LUCID DREAMING: NON-DUAL DREAM YOGA

As you go back to bed and lie down, your level of wakefulness begins to descend.

Level of Wakefulness ←

Begin the process of mental anchoring: 30s of focus, 5s of letting go, and so on.

As you let go more and more, your consciousness begins to descend toward the thredshold between wakefulness and sleep, eventually crossing it (falling asleep).

Beyond this point, there are periods where you briefly shift between wakefulness and sleep.

Threshold between wakefulness and sleep

You are asleep and enter into a dream.

Due to the mental anchoring, you will regain waking consciousness at some point. Because you are in a dream, you will regain waking consciousness within the dream state instead of in the waking state.

66

Don't expect to achieve lucidity on the first few attempts. As you get better at performing this method, you will be able to let your mind drift deeper into sleep without losing consciousness; you will be able to see full and detailed dream imagery through the periphery of your awareness. This method requires practice and dedication, but you can surely achieve it with perseverance. Inducing lucidity from within the dream state with mental anchoring (5b) is my favorite method of becoming lucid in a dream.

Lucid dreaming that's initiated from the dream state will compose as much as 80% to 90% of your lucid dreaming experiences. However, there's also the possibility of directly bridging wakefulness into dream-consciousness.

Although this is a rare event, it is more prone to occur if you are an experienced meditator and have been practicing for some years. It is the art of consciously falling asleep.

Consciously Falling Asleep

To directly go from wakefulness to the dream state without lapsing into unconsciousness, you need to be a mature spiritual practitioner who has expanded their baseline level of consciousness into broader spectrums within subconsciousness.

If your waking consciousness only functions within the parameters of wakefulness (which obviously is its intended purpose), whenever you snap out of the waking state, "you" (the "I" you identify yourself as) will lose consciousness. However, if you have performed spiritual practices such as Kriya Yoga, Kundalini Yoga, or Self-Inquiry, you will have broadened your field of conscious awareness. As you begin practicing in the waking state, your body and mind start to relax into a deeper level of consciousness, one that you are not typically aware in, which is generally reserved for the hypnagogic or dream state.

By continuing to perform spiritual practice, your normal level of conscious awareness "expands" to encompass levels where it wasn't previously lucid. This allows you to remain conscious in states where most people will have become unconscious. From an external observer point of view, if someone were to look at and compare your body side-by-side with that of an unconscious person, both would appear unconscious. However, from your point of view, you would be lucid and aware in your internal dimension (your "I" of the waking consciousness would be aware even though it's out of its typical environment of the waking state), while the other person would be totally unconscious (their "I" of the waking state belongs only to the waking state because it hasn't expanded into other deeper states; hence it would be "off").

By this I mean that as a result of spiritual practice, you will be able to access the dream state and be completely lucid directly from sitting spiritual practice without needing to sleep. However, for the purposes of this book and lucid dreaming, we will apply this teaching in a similar way to the previous method where you go to sleep, wake up after 5 to 6 hours, and then go back to sleep. You do everything the same, except that instead of doing step 5*a* or 5*b*, you will do 5*c*, which doesn't require mental anchoring:

5c. As you lay down in bed, stay in the supine position and observe your mind. See the darkness before your eyes and witness any thoughts that may appear. Keep being mindful, and let whatever comes to your mind come, and whatever goes, go.

As you remain aware, dream imagery and mental impressions remnant from your day, hypnagogic lights, or "sacred geometry" type of figures will arise. Don't look directly at them, otherwise they may fade, or you may lose consciousness and be pulled into a dream—just stay aware with your attention around the periphery in an unfocused manner.

Watch these images or lights without centering your vision on them. They will keep evolving, appearing, and disappearing; your mind may also begin to have lots of thoughts and preoccupations or issues concerning events occurring in your life. Don't lose focus, and keep witnessing all of this. You may also experience vibrations all over your body, hear strange noises, feel like your body is floating, and myriad other sensations, but don't let these happenings distract you from your objective. Stay mindful and relaxed.

As your mind progresses through these stages that precede sleep, you may experience a few obstacles, such as an uncontrollable desire to scratch an itch or to move to another position. There has to be a balance here: you shouldn't scratch that itch or move your body, but if you try too hard not to do these things, it will be as much of a hindrance as scratching the itch or moving the body. In that case, do what you feel is the most natural action, but perform it slowly, naturally, and gently. Even the swallowing of saliva may prove to be an obstacle. The best course of action is to lightly take your attention off those things and just focus on witnessing the content (or the lack of it) on the screen of your mind. You should neither fight with nor engage these reflexes; you have to find a balance. It's like your mind/brain is testing you to see whether or not you are unconscious so that it can give your body the order to fall asleep.

Another obstacle to this process is what are typically called hypnogogic jerks or spasms. These are those sudden jolts and involuntary twitches that your body experiences just as it's about to fall asleep. Try your best to ignore them if they occur; see them as a natural process of falling asleep.

If you manage to get through all of this—and this process may take as little as one minute, or as many as dozens of minutes, depending on your current state—you will experience a sudden and sharp falling sensation and/or tingling vibrations. Don't panic. If you react to these sensations with a sudden jerk, your body won't fall asleep. If you manage to stay deeply relaxed but internally attentive, the body will eventually fall asleep.

During all of this, dream imagery will still be playing on your mental screen. Once your body falls asleep, you will lose complete physical sensory input ("external awareness"), and you will get pulled into the current dream imagery. Or, alternatively, you can keep witnessing them and gently "resist" the pull-in by staying as a passive observer. If you manage to resist it passively, new and different images will appear that will attempt to pull your consciousness in. At this point, you can enter into any dream by imagining yourself there, but depending on the stability of your waking consciousness at that moment, a conscious entrance into a chosen dream (rather than being sucked into one) may cause the imagery to disappear. However, this process will become smoother with practice.

If you don't enter into any dream, you will experience a three-dimensional black void, where you can create your own dream imagery and world from scratch through imagination/visualization. Alternatively, you might venture into out-of-body experiences, or even experience a broader expanse of non-perceptive awareness. It's a state of limitless potential.

A common experience that may occur during this whole process is to feel like you are not falling asleep, while in fact, you are already asleep and dreaming that you are trying to fall asleep—you just didn't realize it. If you suspect that you've been there waiting for your body to fall asleep for quite some time already, and nothing happened, try to do a breath-check; you might be surprised. Oftentimes, you will only realize that you were actually already asleep once you wake up, because it's so real and so similar to the waking state that you can get deceived.

A useful trick is to notice whether you are seeing your room, ceiling, or walls even though your eyes are closed. If you are, you are most definitely asleep and dreaming all of this. Seeing through closed eyes is a signal that your waking consciousness has already transcended the liminal boundary between wakefulness and dreaming.

If your body can't seem to totally relax in the supine position in order to fall asleep (the head usually takes longer to relax profoundly), you can try to perform step 5c in the fetal position, or in your preferred sleeping position. Take caution because that position is also the most likely to lead you to unconscious sleep, because of the mental conditioning that you have programmed into your mind and body from years and years of sleeping. Furthermore, regardless of your sleeping position, it's very likely that you will lose consciousness at some point when attempting to fall asleep consciously, only to gain consciousness again later on. Nonetheless, if you successfully pass through this whole process, you will triumphantly enter into the dream state without losing lucidity. It's a massive achievement.

As an alternative method, instead of passively witnessing your mind as your body falls asleep, you can perform an internally-based repetitive motion that keeps your mind awake, such as slowly mentally chanting *Om* over and over again, as your body falls asleep. This also works, but you'll have to keep coming back to the mantra as your attention scatters toward thoughts and dream imagery. As long as your waking consciousness stays awake while your body falls asleep, you will succeed.

Consciously falling asleep is not the conventional lucid dreaming paradigm where the dreamer becomes aware that they are dreaming within a dream. Rather, it's a conscious infusion of the waking consciousness into the realm of dream-subconsciousness without unconscious lapses. It's a lucid phasing-out of physicality into the multiverse dimension of our inner world.

BARELY TOUCHING WAKEFULNESS WITH AN ALARM CLOCK

Technological advances have also given us new and unconventional ways of achieving lucidity. This method consists of using a custom alarm clock to take advantage of a 1/2 second window where lucidity is easily attainable. To achieve this, you need to go to sleep and wake up at the same time for 2 to 3 weeks, using an alarm clock to get your mind and body conditioned to fall asleep and wake up at the same time every day. Then, program the alarm to sound for just a couple of seconds or for 3 beeps[8], about 30 to 45 minutes before your usual wake up time.

---

[8] Conventional alarm clocks usually lack such options, but there are various alarm clock applications on your smartphone that allow this functionality.

You'll need just enough sound to wake you up, but make sure you don't get startled. It's just a little beep to bring you to a state of semi-wakefulness.

As soon as the alarm clock softly beeps, you will wake up, but you mustn't move. What you want to achieve is a state where you awaken, barely gaining waking state consciousness, and then, a few seconds later, you fall asleep again—but keeping lucidity throughout this process. You just need to barely "scratch" wakefulness, as long as it's enough to remember what's happening and what you're trying to achieve (lucid dreaming) but don't get overly excited or enthusiastic, as that will prevent you from instantly falling back asleep.

It's just a matter of waking up in response to the alarm clock (some time before your typical wake-up time to get you into the sweet spot of REM), not moving, relaxing back into sleep, but staying conscious. In no time, you will transition into the dream state, and regardless of whether it's a direction transition, or whether you experience brief lapses of consciousness, the chances of quickly falling into a dream and becoming lucid become much higher.

This can even allow you to come back into a dream that you were previously dreaming, but with lucidity added. Everybody has had an instance where they were dreaming, and some external noise made them suddenly wake up (and even move), and then they realize it's nothing and just go back to sleep, instantly falling asleep and coming back to the same dream. This method uses the same process but takes advantage of doing it consciously.

Summary of the best methods of achieving lucidity:

I) Becoming lucid within dreams exclusively through the practice of reality checks during the day, having a dream journal, recognizing dream signs, etc.

II) Doing *I)* but using the *Sleep - Wake up - Back to Sleep* method to improve the chances of becoming lucid within a dream. *(5a)*

III) Doing *II)* but instead of merely going back to sleep after the 20-minute waking-up-period, using the technique of mental anchoring to become lucid within a dream as you fall asleep. *(5b)*

IV) Doing *II)* but instead of merely going back to sleep after the 20-minute waking up period, staying as the background Witness of your mind, until you fall asleep consciously and directly enter into a dream, without any lapse in consciousness. *(5c)*

V) Doing *I)* and performing the brief alarm clock method.

Achieving lucidity is a major breakthrough in the oneironaut's journey. Now it's time to learn how to stabilize it!

CHAPTER 6

STABILIZING AWARENESS

Knowing how to stabilize your lucidity in a dream is an indispensable skill if you want to achieve spiritual depth through the dream state. There's nothing that will dishearten and frustrate you more than losing lucidity just a few moments after achieving it.

After having constantly performed reality checks throughout the day, only to confirm that you're in the waking state, it is no wonder then, that once a test fails—proving that you're in the dream state—you feel tremendously excited and experience an overwhelming surge of emotions and fervor. Unfortunately, most of the time, this energetic arousal will be counterproductive and will likely lead you to wake up.

Once you become lucid, you have to do your best to remain calm, albeit proper serenity will only come with continuous lucid dream experience. When lucid dreaming becomes "natural," even though it's still exhilarating, it won't destabilize your state. In every lucid dream, the thrill remains, but there's also a sense of tranquility and wellbeing that prevents your emotional environment from destabilizing. Only acquaintance with lucid dreaming can solve this issue.

In order to improve lucid dreaming stability, you have to cultivate emotional detachment regarding everything in the dream. To achieve this, you need *sadhana*—spiritual practice. If you have been doing what you've been taught in the *Real Yoga Series*, you have already acquired a degree of disengagement when it comes to your emotions and thoughts, so this will come easier. If not, you need to start practicing right away, or at the very least, do some simple form of meditation. You have to reach a state where, despite still experiencing emotions, they don't affect your mind.

Initially, when you are too emotionally invested in the dream, you will most probably lose some, if not all, of your lucidity at some point. If you lose yourself doing something in the dream, the chances of getting back into a lucid state are small. If lucidity falls below a certain threshold, it's just a matter of time before you re-identify with your dream role (as a dream character rather than a lucid dream practitioner), and slip back into unconscious dreaming, or just wake up altogether. For example, if an alluring dream character appears within your dreams, it's easy to become mesmerized by their behavior and words and lose a great deal of lucidity.

To become great at lucid dreaming, you must never forget that you're in a dream, despite whatever emotional involvement occurs. Be in the dream, but remember that you're dreaming. When you operate from a higher level of consciousness, your emotions won't disturb your state of being as much (or at all), and thus a high degree of lucidity can be effortlessly maintained even amidst emotional engagement with the dream.

One of the main dilemmas with lucid dreaming is that it's very easy to either fall back into non-lucidity or wake up. This happens because, unlike the density and stability of the waking state, the dream state is very volatile, which means that even though consciousness has contact with a more expansive portion of its limitless potentiality within subconsciousness, it also has a harder time taking total conscious control of its actions and intentions. Additionally, perception is often unstable and subject to swift and abrupt changes, clashing with your brain's habitual sense of logic and rationality.

If you've ever practiced lucid dreaming, you know that the central approach to staying lucid in the dream is to mindfully immerse yourself in the dream-senses. By doing this, you will stabilize your lucid dream (your physical body will stay asleep).

On the other hand, if you inattentively engage with the dream world, losing yourself in its perceptions, sensations, colors, sounds, etc., you will become so absorbed by them that you will lose lucidity—you become unaware that you are dreaming.

If you do the opposite and consciously refrain from engaging with the dream world—stopping, closing your dream-eyes, and just doing nothing—the dream will fade to black and you will wake up in the "external world" (the waking state)[9].

As a spiritual seeker, a similar yet inverted situation happens to you during what people call "real-life": if you lose yourself in the waking state's experiences, perceptions, sensations, colors, sounds, etc., you will lose contact with your inner dimension (i.e., you'll "stabilize" your consciousness in the physical reality).

On the other hand, if you fully and consciously stop engaging

---

[9] In specific circumstances, if you have enough lucidity, you can experience the three-dimensional void by stopping everything within the dream.

with the physical world and senses (i.e., through spiritual practice or meditation), the world will start to fade away and you will wake up to your inner world. However, if you stop engaging with the world, but do so unconsciously, you fall asleep.

The optimal course of action for a lucid dreamer is to thread through both of these instances but in another, better way:

- *Consciously engaging with the dream* but never forgetting that you are dreaming. If you successfully achieve this, you will build up your energy level and lucidity even more as the dream progresses. The initial insight ("I'm dreaming!") is just the first step toward an even deeper awareness of the dream state and of one's own self. This requires alertness and mindfulness. Regularly performing reality checks, even though you already know that you're dreaming, is also a great approach to stay involved with the dream but never forgetting that you are indeed awake in a dream.

- *Consciously stopping all action* to stop the dream from continuing, but instead of waking up, you use the three-dimensional void as a portal for a different dream, or for deeper spiritual purposes[10].

---

[10] This will be addressed in a later chapter.

Furthermore, there are a couple of things you can do that improve your lucidity and dream stability:

Looking at your dream hands, even though they may be changing, is a great way to stabilize the dream. This is not about performing the hand-check, but just about loading your visual perception with something that is always available (consciously using a dream sense to perceive dream content). Besides looking at your hands, touch them to one another; rub or massage them. It's easy to do and helps immensely in terms of stabilizing lucidity.

You already know that engaging with the dream senses helps to improve stabilization; the visual and tactile dream senses are the strongest for grounding your awareness within the dream body—this method uses both.

You can also use the well-known spinning technique, where you start spinning your dream body; the experience of spinning will also stabilize the dream world.

Either of these two methods can be practiced as soon as you are lucid; they will enable you to improve and stabilize lucidity and have a more profound lucid dream. You can also do them if you notice that your dream is fading or your dream senses are becoming numb; if you feel like you're on the verge of losing lucidity; or if you need to boost the dream's vividness.

If you fail to stabilize the lucid dream and unintentionally wake up, you can get back into the dream if you feel like it's still unfinished. To accomplish this, as soon as you wake up, don't move, keep your eyes closed, and begin remembering the dream, focusing on what was happening. As you do this process of focusing on the dream without moving or thinking about your physical body, you will begin drifting back into sleep, and if you remain alert, you will soon find yourself lucid in your dream once again. You may also experience a short lapse of consciousness during this process, but because you were lucid moments ago, you will regain lucidity more easily. This shares some principles with the method of using a custom alarm clock.

Prolonging your lucidity through its stabilization is directly correlated to an increase in your ability to explore further into the depths of your subconscious, where many treasures and revelations are waiting to be uncovered.

Imagine that you're exploring a distant planet with a special suit that gives you all the life support you require. However, the distance you can explore is limited by your rover's solar-powered battery; it can only receive and store a limited amount of solar energy. Stability in a lucid dream is like that solar-powered battery; if you can increase its storage power, you can explore further reaches on that planet and discover its wonders. If you have a small battery, you always have to go back without venturing too deeply into the unknown. Stabilizing lucidity is the way to increase your lucid dream "battery."

As your skills for maintaining lucidity and dream stability improve, your lucid dreams will become much more powerful and important for your spiritual path. Interaction with dream characters, experiences with collective archetypes, subconscious exploration, and profound spiritual practice, among other things, all become within the realm of possibility. That's the next step.

CHAPTER 7

TRANSFORMING THE SOURCE CODE

Now that you're able to stabilize your awareness in lucid dreams, you will use them to progress along your spiritual path. Many lucid dreamers use this newly acquired skill to have fun in the dream state, and there's nothing wrong with that. However, you should not expect to progress spiritually by merely using dreams to create and fulfill fantasies, develop supernatural dream powers, or rule over the dreams.

You can utilize the stabilized lucid dream state to overcome blockages or hindrances in the subconscious mind, including those seemingly intractable behaviors, thoughts, actions, trauma, or patterns that occur within your daily life or mind that prevent you from progressing further in your spiritual journey. For this, there are different spiritual practices that will need to be done within the dream state.

Whenever someone experiences something painful, they

typically repress those memories, sensations, feelings, emotions, and experiences into the hidden recesses of their mind. But to advance on your spiritual journey, you must deal with those obstacles and erase their power over you, either by coming face to face with them when they manifest (doing so from the vantage point of a higher state of consciousness); or by preventing them from arising altogether, "destroying" them in their unmanifested seed forms before sprouting.

Although this process of purification is usually done through spiritual practice/meditation, it can also be done in the dream state[11]. Opening the hidden reservoir of repressed emotions, feelings, memories, and experiences is indeed a painful thing, but if we stay in the dark concerning these blockages, we are self-sabotaging our own progress. This reservoir doesn't want to be opened and wants to keep you blind because its contents are seemingly incompatible with your conscious personality and behaviors, though your very identity is invisibly shaped by these hidden contents.

---

[11] However, to be successful, your lifestyle will also require some changes. For example, if you perform the same mechanical activity or think about the same thing every day, your dreams will reflect that pattern, which can become an obstacle. Lucidity must also be infused into your daily lifestyle in order to use lucid dreaming for deeper spiritual purposes. This includes being self-conscious in one's daily life and smoothing out anything that you feel blocks you in your dreams.

If you go into dreams with enough spiritual maturity and with the attitude of using them to progress on your spiritual path, they will become authentic spiritual dojos.

THE MATERIALIZATION PRACTICE

This practice consists of allowing your blockages to manifest, enabling you to deal with and overcome them in the dream state.

Once you are lucid and well stabilized in a dream, you should find a clear location where there are neither dream characters nor too much "dream content." A wide, more or less empty place is the best.

Once you are in such a place, sit down in a meditative pose, look to the sky, and shout: "Show me what's currently blocking my spiritual progress!" or "Show me what I must focus on to progress spiritually!"

Once you do this, wait for something to manifest. It could be anything. Don't be scared, but face it with the confidence that this is a dream and nothing terrible can occur—only spiritual purification.

Numerous years ago, when I performed this practice, here's what happened:

Never go into a cavern alone. These words rang through my mind as I heard a strange noise in the deep darkness that lay ahead.

"What am I doing in a cave anyway?" I thought to myself.

But I ignored my own attempt at self-awareness and kept going.

Unfortunately, I couldn't see anything further than a stone's throw away in any direction due to the darkness that pervaded this cavern.

"How do I even know if it's a cavern? I can't see squat." I pondered.

I tried hard to recollect what brought me to this cave, and it was then that I realized:

"I am dreaming."

Once I recognized that I was dreaming, I looked up and saw the sunlight penetrating through an opening at the top of the cave. "This wasn't there before," I realized.

This cave was an expression of my non-lucid subconsciousness, and lucidity was materialized as an opening in the cave where sunlight (awareness) penetrated.

I rubbed my hands attentively, feeling every tactile

sensation increasing my dream lucidity; I performed a breath-check and confirmed that I was dreaming. With this, my dream awareness rose tenfold.

My eyes gazed at the opening bathed by sunlight, and I jumped right through it. As soon as I reached the top, the hole toward the cave closed and I landed firmly on rocky ground. There was nothing on the surface, so the idea of performing the Materialization Practice arose in my mind. I sat down, looked up toward the sky, and shouted: "Show me what I must focus on to progress spiritually!"

I closed my eyes for a few seconds, and when I opened them, there was no visible change. Nothing happened; everything was still the same. This was strange because I had done this practice before and I had seen new things once I opened my eyes after making such a request.

This puzzled me for a while, so I decided to search throughout all of the dream landscape to see if I could find anything. However, all I could find was *nothing*—everything was empty.

It was only after writing this down in my dream journal that I realized that I was shown exactly what I had requested: nothingness/emptiness. What was I supposed to focus on? On being nothing and empty. That was the message.

This shows that even if you don't initially understand the messages you receive in the dream state, it doesn't mean that you won't realize their profound insights later on, even in the waking state—you just need to be mindful enough to grasp them.

THE MIRROR PRACTICE

This practice consists of finding or materializing a special mirror that allows you to see your highest desires. By seeing your current highest subconscious desires, you will unmistakably know whether or not enlightenment is your highest purpose right now.

During the day, but especially before sleeping, you will need to remind yourself that when you're going to dream, you're going to be lucid and do the Mirror Practice.

Whenever you find yourself lucid in a dream and remember to perform the Mirror Practice, you'll need to search for a mirror, or if possible, materialize one. Because you have set the pre-existing intention regarding this lucid dream, you will surely find one within the dream. Even if you can't materialize one right in front of you, your subconscious mind's creative powers will materialize one for you to find.

Once you see it, look deeply into it and confidently affirm: "Show me my biggest desire."

At first, the mirror may be clear, showing no image, or even showing a distorted image that you can't accurately perceive; you must continue to focus on it with the intention of showing you your biggest desire(s). Soon enough, it will reveal what you need to see.

This will allow you to contemplate on your current life's choices and priorities. What is it that you truly want? Do you want to reach liberation from the ego and suffering, and bathe in eternal happiness, or is some mundane desire blocking you from achieving your higher purpose?

Once a month, or a few times a year, you can perform this practice and check the mirror to see what your subconscious shows you. By doing this, you can identify where you are on your path regarding your spiritual progress. As long as you see ordinary desires in the mirror, you will know what you have to work on.

If one day you see emptiness/nothingness when you look at the mirror (this is not the same as the mirror being "clear" and showing no reflection[12]), you can let yourself be absorbed

---

[12] A clear mirror showing no reflection may signify that transcending your identity, persona, or sense of separation is your biggest desire, which is a great motivator to confirm that you're on the right path.

by it, and then stay in that emptiness or nothingness without losing consciousness. This is a potent spiritual practice that overcomes waking/dreaming/sleeping boundaries because it allows you to abide in awareness without content or objects. In such an instance, the mirror is pulling you closer to your original nature—you just have to surrender to it.

The Gladiator of the Subconscious Mind

A powerful and quite simple method to spiritually progress within the dream state is to directly order your subconscious mind to let everything go until only the Truth remains. This has to be commanded with assertiveness.

As soon as you have stabilized your lucidity, look up to the sky and assertively shout:

"I am talking to my subconscious mind! I want all illusions, fears, and lies to fall away right now. I am talking to my subconscious mind. Let everything fall away right now! It is the end of separateness, the end of the 'I-ego!' Only the Truth shall remain."

Repeat this over and over again.

If this is done correctly, what will typically ensue is that the dream state will begin to collapse. A massive windstorm will arise, followed by a thunderstorm with powerful lightning, annihilating everything in the dream state. I've experienced this dozens of times.

As soon as the dream starts falling apart, you must not succumb to fear, although you probably will the first few times. Instead, take a deep breath and focus on your own presence. Notice your presence (it will be easier to become aware of it if you've done presence/consciousness-based practices in the waking state), and hold on to it as if your life depended on it.

The mind will try to "scare" you away by destroying everything in the dream, as an attempt to break you down and wake you up. In some instances, it can even materialize your biggest fears right in front of you.

If you successfully persist by holding on to your presence, the whole dream will fall to pieces, including your dream body. There will be nothing left—but your presence will be present. You will be present—aware—in nothingness.

If you want, while the dream is collapsing, continue shouting "Let everything fall right now! It is the end of separateness, the end of the 'I-ego!' Only the Truth shall remain," over and over again, until there's no more "I" to shout. Then, become aware of your presence. If you become aware of your presence too late, you will wake up.

If you surrender to the fear, even if just for a microsecond, one of these three things will occur:

- This current dream will become a nightmare;

- You will lose lucidity and fall into a new dream;

- You will wake up.

It is just a dream, so there's nothing to fear—but the results, if successful, can be remarkable. If you perform this deceivingly simple practice every time you become lucid in a dream, you will progress spiritually must faster, because it causes a deep change in all aspects of the mind. Despite being lucid, you will feel like you're dying; not you, but everything you once believed was you. This is proper spiritual work.

> "I must not fear. Fear is the mind-killer. Fear is the little-death that brings total obliteration. I will face my fear. I will permit it to pass over me and through me. And when it has gone past I will turn the inner eye to see its path. Where the fear has gone there will be nothing. Only I will remain."
>
> - Frank Herbert
> Dune

INTERACTING WITH DREAM CHARACTERS

Dream characters are those beings that populate our dreams. When someone has a non-lucid dream, they interact with all sorts of dream characters, ranging from those who resemble living persons that they know, to those totally unknown or not even human.

When we lucid dream, we don't consciously interact with dream characters unless we have a purpose. The main reason for this is that it can be hugely distracting, and if the conversation goes on aimlessly, you may lose lucidity.

When you are lucid and encounter dream characters, your interaction will fall into one of these three categories:

1) The dream character completely ignores you or doesn't even perceive your presence. It's as if you were invisible to them. They may represent unconscious parts of your mind.

2) The dream character engages and talks to you, but they seem ignorant of the fact that this is a dream. These characters may also represent unconscious parts of your mind.

3) The dream character possesses a different kind of awareness. They are aware of the dream situation and may have an even higher degree of lucidity than the lucid dreamer. These beings can guide you in the dream or even along your

spiritual path. They may represent deeper parts of your mind, being symbolic of your higher state of consciousness.

There's also a special type of beings that belong to this third category, but they represent the "collective unconscious" of humankind (or of a broader spectrum of consciousness). In other words, they are archetypal figures that dwell as thought-energy forms embedded in humanity's unified mental substratum. They can be accessed because all of our minds are interconnected via this impersonal layer.

Archetypal energy can manifest as various forms in your dreams, depending on your predisposition, cultural background, beliefs, tendencies, etc. These thought-energy forms get infused into your individual mind, having been filtered through your specific "prism." For example, spiritual aspirants may experience the divine archetype (i.e., that which we believe is the embodiment of enlightenment and wisdom) through the figure of Angels, Gods, Devas, Elohim, spirits, the Divine Mother, or even through beings such as Jesus of Nazareth, Gautama Buddha, the prophet Muhammad, Moses, Krishna, or Mahavatar Babaji. In other words, two people may experience the same teaching or archetypal energy within the dream state by way of a completely different expression.

When you are lucid in a dream, a dream character will typically not go out of their way to interact with you. If they do, then you should listen to them, as they may have valuable information or an active task for you. Furthermore, regardless of the dream character's level of awareness, all three types of encounters have the possibility of providing you with some form of insight.

Recurring dream characters may also be representations of unconscious patterns that need to be looked at; by knowing this, you can try to engage with them and alter their dream behavior, subsequently modifying your subconscious programming.

Examples of all Three Types of Dream Characters

1) Representation of an Unconscious Negative Trait

Bill is an assiduous lucid dreamer. He likes to use lucid dreaming as a tool for self-exploration and transcendence.

One day, in a lucid dream, he notices that a dream character seems to be constantly cleaning everything in sight. Bill remembers that he has seen this character before in previous dreams, but didn't think much of it. This time, after giving it some thought, Bill decides to observe this character's behavior more closely and notices that they are living in a state of constant anxiety, fueled by a compulsion to have everything super immaculate.

As he sees this, Bill has the sudden insight that this is a symbol for his own constant anxiety and obsession with needing to have everything clean.

Bill lived a very tough childhood, and the house that he grew up in was always dirty. Thus, unconsciously, he finds that keeping everything super clean—obsessively clean—also keeps his traumatic, negative memories of childhood at bay. What Bill doesn't know yet is that this unconscious pattern is not only bad for his mental well-being but is also what binds him to his trauma and blocks him from going further on his path. A part of his identity and personal story—which causes him tremendous suffering—lay attached to this childhood issue.

So, after understanding what is going on with this dream character, Bill resolves to talk to them. But this dream character ignores him; it's as if they don't see him.

Bill then realizes that this is because he was previously unaware of this negative trait. This was an unconscious and compulsive behavior that he wasn't aware of, and that's why the dream character can't see him. However, as soon as Bill realizes this, the dream character suddenly acquires a different awareness and begins engaging with him.

Bill tells the dream character that he understands their purpose, but now it's time to go so that he can make peace with his childhood and transcend this blockage. The dream character smiles, and the dreamer wakes up.

Things have changed. Bill feels relief; he doesn't feel the weight of compulsively needing to clean anymore, and he smiles. The subconscious trauma has been dissolved.

2) Representation of Current Life Choices and Direction

Diana wants to progress spiritually and achieve liberation from suffering once and for all. She wants enlightenment. Nevertheless, some of her life's choices don't seem to be leading her in that direction.

One day she dreams that she's going to hang out with some friends when she receives a call from The Buddha. As she looks at the Caller ID on her mobile phone, she overhears her friends say in the background, "Let's go, you'll talk to him later," and she doesn't answer The Buddha's phone call.

These friends in the dream state are representational of the lifestyle she's currently leading that is pushing her further away from enlightenment. These dream characters do talk and engage with Diana, but they are ignorant of the state of reality they are in (it's a dream). They are the perfect metaphor for the direction her life is taking—away from The Buddha, away from awakening, away from enlightenment. She ends up going with them to a casino to play roulette.

If Diana were to become lucid, she'd have a better discernment: she could refuse to go with those dream characters and instead accept The Buddha's call. This would reflect a positive change in her life. Those people weren't really her friends, but instead were facets of her own ego. Were she to have accepted The Buddha's call, they would have become jealous and began to shout at her, scared that her predilection toward The Buddha would diminish their power over her (the ego's power over her). They might try to bring her back to their side by making her feel judged or inferior, etc.

When you have a lucid dream, you have to pay special attention to what the dream and its characters are trying to tell you. They may be giving you a message, an insight, or trying to help you see where you're going with your life's choices.

3) Dream Characters with a Higher Awareness

In lucid dreams, there are dream characters that will purposefully lead you to do something spiritually relevant. This can occur in many different manners.

These dream beings have a different presence around them, and when you engage with them, it's as if you become more lucid and the dream state more stable. They are indispensable guides on your dream journey.

Whenever you become aware of a dream character with higher awareness (you will notice a different type of "quality" to them, or they will directly engage with you), you should talk to them and ask some or all of the following questions:

-Who are you?

-What do you represent?

-What's your teaching?

-What am I supposed to do in this dream?

-Show me what I need to know or how to fulfill this dream's objective.

Depending on what they answer (and don't expect to get clear and detailed answers on all of your questions), you have to assess where to proceed with the dream. This is unpredictable—anything can happen—but should you require help, don't shy away from asking them for assistance.

These beings function as representations of higher forms of intelligence that typically lay within higher parts of our mind, or in the collective field of humanity's consciousness (or beyond). In rare instances, they may be symbolic manifestations of the universal mind. They can be archetypes that express themselves in a manner for which you will understand their purpose, embodying the fundamental characteristics of a teaching or energy. Their manifested form/body always depends on the predispositions and cultural background of the one seeing them.

Fundamentally, all three types of dream characters have something useful to teach you; it's up to you to penetrate their appearance and discover the essence of their spiritual transmission.

THE WITNESS OF DREAMS

There are dreams where you don't seem to be participating but are merely a passive observer. In those dreams, without an apparent subject, you are either an invisible figurant or a spectator of the dream's play. These kinds of dreams are rarer and more difficult to achieve lucidity, or even remember.

Basically, you are disembodied from a personal or individual point of view, but you, as the mind, are still actively manifesting and "playing out" the dream. The dream is always you, but in this circumstance, you lack an individual dream body. In other words, your point of attention from where you appear to perceive the world is not centered into any particular body, but is "free floating" as an all-pervading bodiless speck of consciousness. You are in the dream, but don't really belong to it.

To achieve this state consciously, you will need to have practiced Background Witnessing[13] extensively in the waking state, so that you can "switch" from being an active participant in the dream state to the passive disembodied background witness. This is particularly hard to achieve, and besides requiring that you have done extensive sadhana with this type of practice, you should also use the *Wake Back To Bed* method.

Through this method, during the span between the time you awaken, and while you are waiting to go back to bed, you must sit down and witness whatever is in your mind, merely observing the coming and going of thoughts and images, with attention but without attachment. This will improve your chances of achieving this passive yet alert background state when you fall asleep and enter into a dream. Although initially, active participation within the dream is almost a

---

[13] This practice may assume different names and slight variations, according to the tradition or spiritual school and system. This is addressed in detail in the *Real Yoga Series*.

guaranteed requirement in order to become lucid, you can become lucid as a "dream character" and make the switch to the background witness if you have mastered all of the aforementioned.

However, there's an interesting phenomenon. If you pay close attention, you will notice that when dreaming, even when you have an identification with a dream body, you are still observing the whole dream. This means that when you dream, you as consciousness are experiencing individuality through a dream body, but are also simultaneously experiencing the dream as a bodiless witnessing consciousness[14]. This realization is what allows you to switch from being an active participant in the dream to the background witnessing consciousness.

Being lucid in a dream while bodiless, you can witness the dream world and its contents. You are like a bodiless speck of consciousness that is witnessing the dream from the background—an empty screen that is able to watch the unfolding of a movie played on itself. Still, you have to stay alert; lest you begin to identify too much with the plot of the dream, and you suddenly find yourself as a character in it and lose your lucidity.

---

[14] In fact, this background witnessing consciousness "occurs" at all times.

The attainment of this state can also happen spontaneously during the dream, or the dream itself may even begin from this bodiless witnessing point of view. The latter is more likely to occur; everybody has had a dream where they are aware but uninvolved in the dream—they're just witnessing the dream unfold. The difference lies in the fact that you are totally conscious of this, and use it for a spiritual purpose, rather than being in a state of partial lucidity.

Witnessing dreams passively but consciously in the background can be an enlightening practice. If you've read my previous books, you know how crucial background witnessing is to enlightenment. Therefore, it is no surprise that applying it to the dream state can also bring remarkable results.

Witnessing without being sucked into the dream's narrative, aside from the obvious reinforcement of mindfulness and critical observing, helps to create strong dispassion toward the dream content, disengaging emotion from whatever is happening. This is a useful skill that also floods into the waking state. Additionally, by separating your awareness from its contents, you learn how to more easily abide in objectless awareness, which is a critical late-stage practice for enlightenment.

Since the dream world and environment are a reflection of your mind, the continued practice of this technique also gives rise to new insight regarding your subconscious, ego, dream world, state, and all their unfolding.

Furthermore, this can also be a great practice in the sense of giving the ego the keys to the control of the dream, but staying passively aware, observing the dream, and gaining insight into how your subconscious drives, limiting beliefs, and ego-based desires function and express themselves. However, you'll have to be extremely alert because lucidity will be in constant danger of being sucked into pleasurable, semi-conscious experiences.

Armed with this knowledge, you will advance on your spiritual path with higher wisdom and maturity.

Enlightening Nightmares

Nightmares are a common experience; everyone has had them. However, when you use lucid dreaming for spiritual purposes, you'll seldom experience what is actually classified as "nightmare" (i.e., a highly frightening dream).

As you explore your mind through lucid dreaming, you'll be faced with some less pleasing aspects of your identity. But are these nightmares? The word "nightmare" is composed of *Night* plus *Mare*, and the latter means "evil spirit that suffocates people when they sleep." Negative psychological aspects of your identity (i.e., facets that seemingly block the realization of the true Self) are not evil spirits, and facing them is not suffocating. You will need to purify those aspects in order to advance further along your spiritual path—but that's a good thing, not a bad thing.

In non-lucid dreaming, nightmares can be terrifying; they can trigger an intense instinctive emotional response or an acute stress response, which may bring the dream to a sudden end, or conversely, "trap" you in it. However, in lucid dreaming, nightmares can transform into enlightening dreams if they're approached with the right lucidity and mindset.

You have to recontextualize nightmares as dreams that show you things that you need to accept, purify, and transcend by letting go; you'll be confronting and purifying negative psychological imprints that manifest as subconscious illusions.

If you encounter eerie entities or experience frightening dreams while lucid, remind yourself that you're in a dream, and try to understand why what is happening is happening so that you can overcome it.

As you purify your mind, it will become more "transparent," which allows you to probe deeper into yourself with less obtrusive mental or psychological impressions (i.e., samskaras). This is not to say that you won't encounter a vast range of adverse somatic and psychological experiences (within the dream and afterward), but they will pass. Be alert and use these moments as ways to exercise your power of mindfulness and discernment.

If you're not yet at the level where you can successfully do the aforementioned, and you experience a "nightmare," don't run from it or attempt to wake up. Escaping from it won't eliminate it, because it will occur again in one form or another. Instead, accept the current state of the dream and affirm: "This is a dream, you can't do anything. You're just an illusion. I am pure light—I am pure Consciousness." More than just saying it, feel it. Embrace the darkness with light, or surrender to a higher power (i.e., God, pure Consciousness, Absolute, etc.), and watch that nightmare dissolve into light.

Facing your biggest fears in a dream may sound scary, but know that if you approach them with lucidity, it'll be a transformative moment. Transforming a "nightmare-dream" into an "enlightening-dream" is a mesmerizing experience; it will infuse your dream body with divine light, profound inner peace, and a powerful sense of having accomplished something immense.

In the end, it is up to you to decide whether a dream is a nightmare—or a chance to integrate and transcend some of your identity's darkest aspects.

CHAPTER 8

CONVENTIONAL SPIRITUAL PRACTICE WITHIN THE DREAM STATE

Many of the practices that can be done in the waking state can also be done in the dream state. To do so, you need some degree of experience with both lucid dreaming and waking state spiritual sadhana. The dream state is very volatile, but it's also exceptional for spiritual practice; because we are in the subconscious space, things are "on steroids." This means that all effects are stronger and easier to achieve, but paradoxically, also harder to sustain and make permanent.

If you are reading this book, you probably already do some form of spiritual practice, such as Kriya Yoga, Kundalini Yoga, or some type of meditation. All of these can also be done in the dream state, you just have to be attentive to the volatility of the dream, and to the stronger and more instantaneous effects.

As explained in *Yogic Dharma*, in the chapter entitled "Spiritual Practice is the Golden Shining Jewel":

> "Spiritual practice is the employment of our body, mind, and awareness in a methodical and practical manner for the purpose of achieving a deeper state of consciousness that allows one to gain insight into and then abide as one's essence. It is the endeavor of finding out who we truly are. We are using our individual consciousness to go beyond its narrow field of awareness into a broader and more expansive universal awareness where we realize our inherent unity with the Cosmos. In other words, we are attempting to go from being a person (limited individual consciousness) to being God (unlimited universal consciousness). Meditation, spiritual practice or *sadhana* is the ultimate form of activity."

Performing waking state spiritual practice in the dream state has the same premise; the main difference is your attention and concentration level. Whenever you practice in the waking state, if you lose your attention, you gently come back to the practice and focus on what you are supposed to be focusing on. However, in the dream state, if you lose attention, you can easily slip into non-lucidity or suddenly find yourself on a whole new dream.

To prevent destabilization, you can perform your practices with your dream eyes opened; or as you do them, you can rub your hands together once in a while to keep yourself grounded into the dream. In the waking state, this would pose a big distraction, disrupting your concentration and the stillness of your physical body; however, in the dream state, this is not the case, because your attention can reach heightened levels quite quickly, and the body is a dream body, therefore its stillness is irrelevant. Furthermore, with time, this gets smoother.

Before practicing standard waking state sadhana in the dream world, you should find or create a proper place for spiritual practice (in the dream). Use this same space every time you perform waking state spiritual practice in the dream state, as it reinforces your mental conditioning and dream stabilization.

If you perform spiritual practices that use the breath as an object of concentration, you should strive to do them with the subtle form of the breath, *prana*, instead of with the actual breath itself. Aside from being a deeper version of the practice and not constrained to the physical limitations that are typically present, breath-related practices performed in the dream world can sometimes affect your breathing patterns in your physical body. In other words, if you happen to restrain your breath in the dream state repeatedly through a spiritual practice, there's a chance that your physical body will start to mimic this same breathing pattern, causing you to wake up. Using prana as the object of meditation instead of the breath is a fail-safe way to prevent you from waking up.

In the waking state, people only notice that they are breathing if they pay attention to their breath. In the dream state, breathing is never noticed (doesn't even occur) until you pay attention to it, just like in the waking state. But since there is no need to breathe there, this happens just out of habit.

If you do a breath-related practice such as the classic Kriya Pranayama, instead of inhaling and exhaling air, just perform the practice as if you don't need to breathe: sense, feel, and visualize pranic energy running up and down through the spinal cord.

If you're performing a mindfulness-of-breathing practice, instead of witnessing the in-breath and the out-breath, you will witness pranic energy in place of the breathing. Essentially, it is about using prana/energy as the object of concentration instead of air.

By performing practices directly with prana, we are also more prone to activating Kundalini energy and experiencing powerful blissful states[15]. In waking state sadhanas, breath works as an indirect way of controlling prana and awakening sensitivity to it. By removing the intermediary, we are basically capable of performing practices akin to being in the breathless state[16].

Now the question may arise: can spiritual practice done in lucid dreams (i.e., Dream Yoga) be used as the sole practice for enlightenment, or should it be used as an auxiliary method?

It could be used as the main practice, but in the overwhelming majority of cases, it should be used as a supplemental practice.

Moreover, until you become proficient at achieving lucidity, Dream Yoga practice can be disruptive to daily life and hinder your ability to fulfill your worldly responsibilities because it may mess up your sleep cycles, making you sleep deprived.

---

[15] When you perform Kundalini activating techniques or practices that involve sexual energy manipulation in the dream state, you may experience different types of raptures and orgasmic pleasures, sometimes with effects persisting for days or weeks.

[16] Breathlessness is called *Kevala Kumbhaka*. When, through some yogic practices, the in-breath merges with the out-breath, they cancel each other out and breathlessness occurs. There is no breathing in the dream state, so if you perform a breath-based yogic practice, you are essentially starting from a breathless point, and though it's different from Kevala Khumbhaka, you can swiftly achieve a similar state.

The truth of the matter is that most people's lifestyles today are not compatible with the consistent practice of lucid dreaming or Dream Yoga, which means that most seekers would do better focusing their energy on performing their primary practices during the waking hours.

As an auxiliary practice, lucid dreaming can fit into most people's lifestyles. It can be practiced or attempted whenever you don't have a predetermined hour to wake up the following day, or during vacations, retreats, etc. Even though your progression will be much slower than if you were practicing it every day, it's still very useful for your spiritual advancement.

By reading this chapter, you may wind up with the idea that performing waking state spiritual practice within the dream state is a straightforward achievement. However, it is not as easy as it might sound. You do need to be proficient at achieving lucidity and stabilizing it before embarking on these types of practices; otherwise you will wake up pretty easily when you begin doing waking state spiritual practices, as they can be very disruptive to the dream state stability. But don't let this stop you from trying, because if you're successful, it will be one of the most lively and ecstatic adventures you'll ever experience—it is the true beginning of Dream Yoga.

CHAPTER 9

DREAM UNITY AND INSIGHTS

For the typical dreamer, the insights attained while dreaming may not translate right away into conscious knowledge in the waking state. Instead, they may be stored away in the subconscious, and eventually, flourish and manifest in the waking state when the time is right.

The question of how well knowledge, experience, wisdom, or insights gleaned from the dream state are transferred over to the waking state depends on the level of lucidity of the dreamer and how smooth the transition between states is. A connection between dreams and waking life must be established as if both the conscious and subconscious minds worked in unison under the same individual consciousness that exerts the conscious decision-making process. With diligent lucid dreaming practice, this occurs naturally.

When you wake up from a nonlucid dream, there's a transition between your dream-self and the waking-self which may lead to brief disorientation; memories of the dream may be unclear, and if not recollected right away, they will be stored in the corners of the subconscious.

However, this doesn't happen when a lucid dream ends because the waking-self is the one that's lucid within the dream state. Therefore, there's a degree of continuity between lucid dreaming and then waking up in the physical dimension, seeing that the identity attached to the "I" is the same, and thus there's no lapse of consciousness between the end of the dream and the beginning of the waking state. Because there's typically no temporary confusion or lack of dream memories when we wake up lucid from a dream, knowledge, insights, and wisdom are more easily brought to the waking state, bridging both worlds.

A remarkable insight to glean through dream spiritual practice is when you experientially realize that all dream contents are actually you; that everything that you perceive within a dream comes from you. This is true for what is objectively perceived (forms), as they are a manifestation of your mind (*the all* within the dream comes from *the one mind*), and to what is outside of your individual spectrum of consciousness, such as when archetypal energy of the collective mind manifests into your dream.

This is easy to grasp:

When you dream, everything within the dream is composed of contents of your mind; without your mind, there would be no dream. The dream characters, the mountains and valleys, the sun and the moon, and even the thoughts you experience while dreaming—all come from your mind.

Now imagine that a dream character within the dream goes to sleep and dreams. Everything in their dream has been composed by them (their mind), but since that dream character has been created by your mind, everything in their own dream has also been created by your mind. If you wanted that dream character to realize that they were dreaming, and you had the power to do so, you'd manifest in their dream and give them some direction or insight into this realization. Since your mind is the substratum mind of all the dream minds in the dream world, you are the collective mind of all of those beings.

The dream character is you[17], the dream they are having is you, and the collective mind is also you. The same happens in your dreams; even archetypal energies and thought-

---

[17] Even your own dream character/identity/ego/personality is unreal. Failure to recognize this may lead some lucid dreamers to believe that they—the individual experiencer of the dream—are real while other dream characters are unreal. This is a mistake because everything within the dream except consciousness itself is unreal.

forms that you experience that come from the collective mind are also you, but just in another non-individual level.

Considering that, at first, when you dream, things appear to exist independently of your own perception (they appear to exist on their own), you need to acquire a high level of lucidity and directly experience that this is not truly the case—you are all the things; you are one.

If you change the setting from the dream state to the waking state, you will notice that things also appear to exist independently of your perception, which is not really the case. Don't get me wrong; it is true that they exist independently of yourself if you see yourself as an individual being, the "I-ego." But once you go further down the rabbit hole, you realize that everything is interconnected, as one single mind—the universal mind.

Dreams are just like the waking state; if the waking state appears to superimpose itself as a movie on the empty screen of consciousness, the same happens with dreams.

Understand that even though one could say that you're the one dreaming the dream characters in the dream state (they were created by your individual mind), while God is "dreaming" the "dream characters" in the waking state (we are a creation of the universal mind), such an assertion would be made by the ego, because only the ego can feel separated from God. It is either you dreaming them all as God, or God dreaming them all as you. There's no distinction unless you put on the ego's lens of perception.

Both the dream you experience, and you, the dreamer, consist of illusory manifestations of consciousness, but there's a difference: your dream presence also has awareness, which is never an object, but the subject; and it is this very awareness that you must hold on to at a later stage to reach non-dual levels of practice.

As a result of the vast number of lucid dreams that you will experience over time, you will derive numerous insights, some more important than others. There are five fundamental insights, however, that every lucid dreamer or dream yogi will experience throughout his dream sadhana toward enlightenment:

Dreams feel as real as the waking state.

This is probably one of the first insights a lucid dreamer has. Perceptions, sensations, images, sounds, smells, etc., everything feels so real, so solid, so authentic; they are as vivid, if not more so, than in the waking state.

The dream state is composed of unstable illusions and mirages.

However, as time goes by and the lucid dreamer continues practicing more and more, they will notice that despite the apparent realness of the dream state, it is composed of mental content, and is nothing more than unstable mirages—illusions—that come and go. Dream content is like a volatile soap bubble: even the softest of breaths can alter its form—or break it.

My own dream body is an illusion.

Going further, the oneironaut discovers that their own dream body is an illusion, just like every other thing in the dream state. However, the knowing by which they know this is not an illusion, and this is a little key that will help them go further into their own consciousness.

Whenever a dreamer realizes that their consciousness is not really "within" the dream body, but only appears to be so, they gain first-hand knowledge regarding this deceptive mechanism of believing oneself to be the body. Furthermore, as they experience different types or models, more or less similar to their waking state identity, and even among various degrees of lucidity, they realize that even their identity is unreal. This allows them to bring that insight into the waking state, arriving at the same conclusion and ceasing to mistake who they are for their body or identity.

The waking state's perceptions and forms are as unreal as in a dream.

Through spiritual practice, both in the waking and dream state, the dream yogi realizes that the quintessential nature of form and of everything that is perceived by the waking state's senses is as unreal as in the dream state—both states are states of mind. It's not that perception in the dream state is as real as waking state's perception—it's waking state's perception that is as unreal as in a dream.

All states of mind are dual by nature, as they consist of a subject that perceives an object; there's always a relationship (i.e., a division or separation) between both.

It is important to understand that an object cannot ever be separated from perception itself (the object is the perception itself that is being perceived), and perception cannot ever exist without a subject (the dual states of waking or dreaming are always dependent upon the experiencer/perceiver/subject), but there can be a subject without perception (non-dual objectless consciousness; deep dreamless sleep).

The dreamer, therefore, realizing this, abides in its own subjectivity of being—objectless consciousness—and realizes that nothing besides this can be real because, aside from pure consciousness, everything is temporary, transient, and dependent upon a subject of experience. Thus, we arrive at the ultimate Dream Yoga insight that illuminates both the waking and dreaming states:

Dreaming and waking are both dreams.
Only Consciousness is real.

Nothing that appears on the screen of consciousness is real; all images that play on the screen are ephemeral illusions; they are transient movements in the eternity of immutable consciousness.

What do I mean by real? We typically don't consider dreams to be real because they don't exist on their own (without our mind creating them), and due to them being transient or finite (they come and go).

For something to be real, it must not depend on anything but itself to be present, otherwise that other something that allows it to be is more real than the thing itself; and it must be immutable or eternal because change means the end of something and the beginning of something new. In other words, *real* needs omnipresence and eternity.

Unmistakably, both waking and dreaming states are composed of forms and do not fulfill such requisites; they come and go. When you're awake, the dream state is not present within your consciousness; when you're dreaming, the waking state is not present within your consciousness.

Although our mind seems to be self-conscious, it is not, since its primal thought—"I"—is not present in deep dreamless sleep, nor in any so-called *unconscious* state. There's no mind there. We know that it is not present because we know that we experience nothing during those states, which means that we exist, but the knower of objects, the mind, is not there.

The mind also comes (waking and dream states; dual states) and goes (deep sleep/unconsciousness states).

What about pure Consciousness?

Pure Consciousness—consciousness without objects—is the substratum upon which everything can appear and disappear.

For anything to exist, there must be an awareness of it, because nothing is self-existing on its own, except for this primal consciousness. Although nothing can be known without consciousness, consciousness doesn't need anything to exist.

This means that pure Consciousness is self-aware, which means it knows itself without needing any other consciousness to know it.

How then can it be known?

It can't be known. There is no knower of the ultimate Consciousness. The only way to *know* it is to BE it. The ultimate Consciousness knows itself, being.

This means that besides being self-aware, it is also uncreated and beyond time. It was never created, it ever existed, it is immutable and eternal.

If pure Consciousness is omnipresent and eternal, then That, and only That, is what is real. The direct realization of this is the ultimate insight.

CHAPTER 10

NON-DUAL DREAM YOGA

"I am dreaming!"

This is the most awaited moment for any lucid dreaming practitioner. Clarity, energy, joy, and a sense of wonder and magnificence are infused into us once we realize that we're actually in a dream.

What exactly happens once someone realizes that they are dreaming? Who is the realizer of that insight?

As we've seen in chapter 4, *The Illusory Dreamer*, it is the "waking-self" or "waking-ego" that realizes that they are dreaming. At that moment, the "dream-self" or "dream-ego" and its identity (and everything that comes along with it) are partly or entirely discarded and replaced by the waking-self.

However, both the waking-self and the dream-self are facets of the same primordial sense of being a separate self, the "I-ego."

This means that "I am dreaming!" is not only a realization of lucidity but also a realization of separateness.

To advance further in Dream Yoga and to transform it into a non-dual practice that leads you to enlightenment, you will have to turn your attention to the "I" that is dreaming, to your self, even amidst the marvels of the dream state. This should only be attempted once you are proficient in the practice of lucid dreaming. If you try to do it prematurely, after only a couple of months of practice, it will be hard to succeed. Furthermore, waking state sadhana is a definite prerequisite for this.

Upon realizing that you are dreaming, and after stabilizing the dream state, instead of engaging with and focusing on the dream, you will focus on the one who realizes that they are dreaming. Ask yourself:

Who is the "I" that is dreaming?

Who am I, the lucid dreamer?

Can you "locate" it—the "I"?

Be aware of the "I" that you are within that dream; not the identity or the personality, but the sense of "I." This practice requires a high degree of spiritual discernment, since you have to be able to distinguish between the essence of "I" (the feeling of being; your presence) and the contents of "I" (identity, likes, dislikes, memories, ideas, thoughts, etc.).

Don't search for an object or something that can be perceived objectively, because you will find none. "I" is the subject, not an object. Whatever you see or perceive is not "I;" "I" is the seer or the perceiver.

Once you grasp the sense of "I," fall back into that "I" that is lucidly dreaming. Let yourself fall into your background of being. Let everything go—surrender everything into your higher unmanifested intelligence, into your true deathless Self. Relinquish the dream, the dreamer, and the act of dreaming. Let the dream atoms and the necessity of perception fade into nothingness, if required. Just abide in your sense of presence and let everything else disappear.

This inward practice goes beyond the dream state into a subjective state that lies between dream, waking, and unconscious sleep. By abiding with the "I" in the dream state, you will begin to loosen and then eventually cut the knot that seems to bind what is illusory to what is real.

This "falling back into I" is most likely initially felt as an illuminated emptiness or internal spaciousness-nothingness, while everything else begins to dissolve and disappear. You have to let go of the dream and everything in it.

The dissolving of the dream space can occur in two ways:

1. The more intense and powerful the Self-Awareness is, the more the dream fades into nothingness (not blackness, which is perceivable, but non-conceptual emptiness/nothingness). You will lose all sensory experience and dream body-awareness, and everything will disappear. All you have to do is to keep holding onto the awareness of "I" until even the "I" dissolves and you experience "I-less awareness," or until you wake up.

Or

2. If you stop engaging with the dream and continue to be aware of "I," yet instinctively keep the dream in the periphery of your awareness, the dream will revert back to its potential state. In other words, it will be transformed into the primordial soup that gives rise to dreams, the three-dimensional black void[18]. In this situation, your awareness will be drawn to observe the three-dimensional void, and if you become too absorbed into it, a new dream may begin to emerge and you will be sucked into it. If you reach this point, you have to observe the observer of the black three-dimensional void. Don't focus on the void, but on the awareness that is aware

---

[18] Although I refer to it as "black void," it's not black per se; it's more nothingness than black, but black gives a better context of understanding, in case you experience it or in order to help "get there."

of the void. Observing the observer is the same as being aware of "I."

In both of these situations, you must stay aware of "I." That's all that is required.

This is merely remembering your real nature, what is prior to the ego: consciousness devoid of content. The goal of this practice is to remember the lightless light within the dream state. It is the same remembrance that can be achieved in the waking state through non-dual sadhanas, where you are consciously being aware of being objectless consciousness. It is incredibly blissful and peaceful.

This way of approaching Dream Yoga is a breakthrough for the seeker. It is a transforming dual Dream Yoga into non-dual Dream Yoga.

When Dream Lucidity no Longer Matters

It is important to understand that before realizing that you were dreaming, you were not unconscious. How could you possibly be unconscious if you were able to perceive the contents of the dream and inquire whether you were dreaming?

This provides another big realization: prior to becoming lucid, you were not unaware—only the waking-ego, who you take yourself to be, was unaware. With lucidity, only the attributes of the separate self, the ego, changed. But the fact of the matter is that who you take yourself to be is not who you are; it's just a flimsy concept that you have of who you are.

Since it is the waking-ego that becomes lucid, and the waking-ego is but a transient play of consciousness, why does it really matter if it becomes lucid in a dream in the first place? You are aware in every dream, regardless of whether you are lucid or not.

This may seem counter-intuitive at first, especially because I've been emphasizing how imperative lucidity is throughout this book. Yes, lucidity is vital! However, you may reach an advanced point where you will see how this apparent contradiction is, in fact, an essential teaching beyond typical dream lucidity: if your goal is to realize your true nature as consciousness, you must realize that you, as consciousness, are always aware, irrespective of whether you are lucid or not in a dream. What changes is the ego, not the background of consciousness.

The only change with lucidity is the presence of the waking-ego (the identity of the waking state).

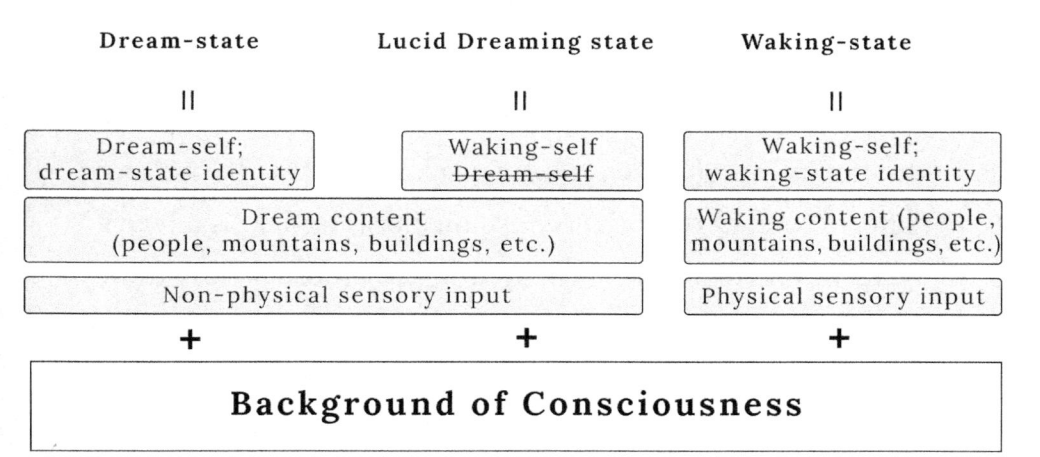

Dream-state	Lucid Dreaming state	Waking-state
=	=	=
Dream-self; dream-state identity	Waking-self; ~~Dream-self~~	Waking-self; waking-state identity
Dream content (people, mountains, buildings, etc.)		Waking content (people, mountains, buildings, etc.)
Non-physical sensory input		Physical sensory input
+	+	+

Background of Consciousness

Consciousness is always conscious

This means that lucid dreaming in and of itself, as is generally known and performed, is irrelevant to enlightenment. However, it is relevant to enlightenment if applied with the purpose of using the dream state to become aware of consciousness itself. This process begins with lucid dreaming, then becomes Dream Yoga, and finally, non-dual Dream Yoga. This is how we turn classic lucid dreaming into non-dual lucid dreaming.

It doesn't matter if you are awake in the dream or not, as long as the dreaming-self "remembers" to become self-aware during the dream state. To achieve this spontaneous Self-Awareness, you need to practice a lot of non-dual

Dream Yoga in order to flood the subconscious with the singular purpose of being contentless consciousness.

The consciousness by which you become aware of consciousness in the dream state is the same consciousness by which you become aware of consciousness in the waking state. There is only one consciousness, and it is always aware of itself. Waking-ego, dream-ego—these all lose their meaning because you know you are neither of these stories! You have lost your identification with any of these dual states.

With profound Self-Awareness, the dream is no longer composed of images or perceptions, but only of consciousness; the dream images and perceptions were actually consciousness, clouded by your mind. Everything is seen as consciousness. At this point, it doesn't make sense calling it a dream anymore, because the dream is within consciousness, and only consciousness is.

If you are at this advanced stage of the spiritual path, and you already perform the non-dual Self-Awareness type of practices (e.g., Kriya Yoga's Parvastha, Kundalini Yoga's post-practice of "just being," Self-inquiry, etc.), this non-dual dream practice is merely an extension of that practice in the waking state.

This is quite an astonishing discovery because you let go of the need to become lucid in dreams, which means that every dream becomes an opportunity for non-dual Self-Awareness. By performing this process, your "I" begins to shed its outer egoic layers, even pertaining to the waking state, regardless of the waking-ego's presence. This is because all facets of the ego, from the waking-ego to the dream-ego, are linked by the "I-ego" itself through "subconscious linkage."

Once non-dual lucid dreaming becomes the norm, you are no longer looking to become lucid in dreams; instead, you want to become self-aware in dreams, regardless of the ego's state of lucidity. This fundamentally changes how you approach lucid dreaming and all forms of Dream Yoga, because the main goal transitions from awakening the waking-ego within dreams to awakening the awareness of being aware of consciousness! This "I-less" awareness is verily the ultimate bliss. It is you.

CHAPTER 11

LIMINAL PHENOMENA AND SIDE-EFFECTS

SLEEP PARALYSIS

One of the most common experiences that lucid dreamers may encounter in their journey toward lucidity, especially those who attempt to fall asleep consciously, is the well-documented *sleep paralysis*.

In this state—body asleep, mind semi-awake in the waking state—you simply can't move. It can be a terrifying experience. As if that weren't enough, because your mind is in a semi-conscious state between wakefulness and dreaming, you can very easily experience vivid hallucinations. When the combination of not being able to move the body merges with intense hallucinations and fear of not knowing what's going on, what ensues is that you may feel that a malevolent presence is pressuring or sitting on your chest or solar plexus area and preventing you from moving. There are countless possible nasty hallucinations that may occur when someone experiences this state, but remember that they're just that—hallucinations.

If you experience sleep paralysis without having any prior knowledge about it, you may become so scared that you'll avoid practicing lucid dreaming or anything like it for a while. This can be exacerbated if you've read about the terrible experiences described in certain folklore or "New-Age" teachings, or if you have a religious or even standard spiritual background that's not based on proper guidance toward self-liberation. However, by reading and learning about sleep paralysis in a more sensible and less dogmatic way, it doesn't have to become an obstacle because you know that despite whatever occurs, nothing serious is really happening to you; they're just vivid hallucinations. While you may initially be startled, you will overcome them because you recognize these hallucinations for what they are without being traumatized.

Sleep paralysis is actually a fabulous state that you can use to enter into dreams with lucidity, by imagining them and seeing yourself there. With this knowledge, sleep paralysis becomes fun. Despite not being able to physically move, you can swirl around up and down in a "non-physical body," and even switch your referential point of perception to an out-of-body location, and move from there.

There's also a trick to get out of sleep paralysis that has always worked for me, in case you need it: try to wiggle your toes as much as you can. Initially, they won't move, but if you try really hard, they will begin to move and then suddenly, your whole body will be able to move.

Nonetheless, sleep paralysis is a great vehicle to induce lucid dreams and to explore the phenomenon of out-of-body projections. Don't be afraid of it, and embrace the opportunity it gives you.

False Awakenings

Sometimes, when a lucid dream ends, you "wake up" in another very convincing dream that mimics the place where you were previously asleep. This is a *false awakening*. It's not the real awakening in physical reality, but seems like it, deluding the dreamer into believing they're actually awake in the waking state.

Some false awakenings can be mentally disruptive because they may trap you in a loop of numerous false awakenings before waking up in the actual "physical reality."

Recognizing a false awakening for what it is may be quite

tricky, since you never realize that you're supposed to question the reality of that state: the dream just ended, and you seem to wake up wherever you were before falling asleep[19]. You may even go about your day, shower, eat, etc., until you notice something offbeat that leads you to realize that you are still dreaming. Sometimes, you may write down a dream in your journal after waking up from a lucid dream, and then go back to sleep, only to find out later that it was a false awakening and there's nothing in your journal—and now you don't remember much of the dream anymore. How disappointing!

Once you realize that you are in a false awakening and wake up, there's a chance that you've just entered into yet in another one. However, you won't be fooled this second time, and you will begin questioning reality with reality-checks such as the breath-check until you know for sure that you are awake in the physical realm.

The best way to stop being trapped within a false awakening is to always perform a reality check once you wake up from a dream. Don't be deceived into believing that it isn't worth it because you are convinced that you are in the real waking state—there won't be any noticeable difference between the

---

[19] Though you may also wake up in a different room, you will believe that you went to sleep in that place.

false awakening and the real awakening in the waking state. Only through further scrutiny will you discover its illusory nature, typically by noticing that there's something different or unusual in the room where you fell asleep.

I was once trapped in a cycle of false awakenings for what seemed to be quite a long time. I went through about ten interactions before waking up in the real physical state. The issue was that once I realized I was in a false awakening, I just kept waking up, over and over again, failing reality check after reality check.

I saw my mind searching for a stable physical reality with a body that it could attach itself to, perusing thousands of false awakening dream realities without knowing for sure which was the actual physical waking one, until suddenly, after waking up ten times, I woke up in the physical reality. It was a fascinating experience.

False awakenings will happen to you; there's no way around it. Always remember to utilize reality checks and critical reasoning to overcome them.

GROUNDING

By virtue of the energetic nature of some sadhanas (i.e., Kundalini Yoga), practitioners may need to release the excess energy by anchoring their consciousness into the physical reality.

Lucid dreaming usually doesn't require as much grounding as those spiritual disciplines because it is done while asleep. However, the continuous practice of lucid dreaming may disrupt your sleeping patterns, possibly affecting your day-to-day responsibilities and general life.

Insufficient amounts of deep dreamless sleep, or continuous poor sleep quality will make anyone tired, groggy, impatient, unable to concentrate, etc.—and can throw one's whole system out of whack. Therefore, you have to be mindful to find the appropriate balance between your daily life, waking and dreaming spiritual practice, and proper sleep[20].

Ideally, after a lot of practice, you'll find an equilibrium in which you naturally have lucid dreams without having to change anything in your sleeping schedule. In theory, this

---

[20] Getting sufficient sleep, eating healthy and nutritious food, engaging in physical exercise, and practicing meditation are well-known factors that contribute to excellent mental and physical health. The same applies to those who practice lucid dreaming.

is possible, but it's hard to put into actual reality, especially considering that after achieving some success with lucid dreaming, you will want to practice more and more often. This may lead you to start changing all of your patterns and schedules in order to maximize your chances of having more and deeper lucid dreams.

Nonetheless, here are some potential side-effects for those who go overboard without having first established a solid meditative foundation and some degree of spiritual maturity:

- You're more prone to having sudden dissociative experiences in the waking state.

- There's a "flooding" of over-sensitivity or sense-enhancement that comes from the subconscious mind and begins to inundate the conscious mind, and you might not be able to cope with that without feeling overwhelmed.

- You may feel as if the waking state doesn't make much sense anymore, and it's not worth fulfilling your daily responsibilities.

- You may become addicted to the ecstasy and rush that are experienced in lucid dreams, and feel that everything else in the waking state seems to no longer stimulate you or give you joy.

To counteract these, you can perform asana-based practices or physical exercise. These will help to ground your energy and mind.

Interacting with nature is also a great way to get grounded. Walking barefoot in a forest, on a beach, or connecting with animals, trees and plants will help you discharge all of the excess energy. This is an easy, peaceful, and joyful way to get grounded. Swimming in the sea also has a similar effect.

There's no doubt that you must harmonize your nocturnal adventures with your daily life, but this requires discernment and a higher degree of consciousness—one that you acquire through proper spiritual practice alongside a balanced lifestyle.

Part 3

CHAPTER 12

THE DREAM OF WAKEFULNESS

Dream Yoga is the raft that helps us cross the rapids of the dream world, giving us the opportunity to realize both the illusory nature of the dream state—and of the waking state by extension—and the real nature of the substratum consciousness that provides the basis for both to occur.

By practicing in our dreams, we realize that the powerful web of Maya is so deceptive and illusory that, unless faced with lucidity, we will be fooled into believing it's true. Once this insight becomes your living experience, you begin to understand the dream-like nature of the waking state—it really is no different. Everything is transient; it appears, takes the spotlight, and then fades into oblivion. As a consequence of this understanding, you begin to lessen the burdens you've been carrying your whole life, for your tensions and problems are no more real than the fabric from which the illusory nature of the waking state has been created.

Our experience of the world occurs through the identification and interpretation of sensory information; but our sense perceptions—just like thought—are not the arbiters of realness. A rock is solid in the waking state, but it can also be solid in the dream state. Its solidity is, therefore, meaningless.

All phenomena are illusions in the sense that they don't exist on their own without a consciousness to perceive them. The sensory impressions of everything we perceive occur through the workings of the mind and brain, both in the waking and dream state. While it may seem like we perceive things that exist on their own, as objective and independent objects, this is not actually the case, just like in a dream. This is the experience of everyone. Even the line of thought, "I filmed you with a camera while you were unconscious, so now you see that the world exists while you were not aware of it, independently of you" is a false proposition because to know this, consciousness has to be present beforehand.

It is only after waking up ("activating" waking state consciousness) that you can see the video that supposedly shows that the world existed independently of your own consciousness.

This exact scenario could occur during a dream. In fact, I've had countless dreams where I went to sleep and woke up the next day *within the dream*; I've had dreams where I had memories of a childhood I never experienced; I've had dreams where world-changing dream events occurred while I was sleeping within the dream, and I only found out about them when I woke up the next day, in the dream. I've even had dreams where a dream character was trying to show me that the reality we were in—a dream, unbeknownst to him—was real and existed independently of my own consciousness. It was funny because I was fully aware that it was a dream, yet I was seeing someone trying to decipher the nature of reality with logic, "dream-tools," "dream-senses," and "dream-laws." Guess what? This dream character even attempted to convince me by using the example of the video camera recording me while I was sleeping. Somehow, it is a reminder of the state of the waking world we currently live in, where the evidence presented by the senses seems to be the absolute arbiter of reality.

When you're dreaming, you're convinced that you're awake and objectively experiencing "actual" reality. It is only after becoming lucid or returning to wakefulness that you realize that it was all an illusion. Most people make the same assumption in the waking state.

But how do you know when you are really awake? Sense perceptions, logical thoughts, or intuition are not enough because all of these can be experienced in the same precise manner in the dream state. Are you awake right now? This question is not posed as to whether you are awake in the physical body in the physical reality, since all bodies and realities seem physical while we are nonlucid—but as whether you are really *awake* or *asleep*.

What is being awake? To be awake is to be aware of what is *Real* instead of an illusion.

If dreams are illusions because they are transient and don't exist on their own, so is the waking state. They're not what is Real. Throughout this book, you've already learned about what is Real—pure Consciousness. This is the crux of all spirituality[21].

Consciousness is what typically escapes our attention, and even the vast majority of experienced lucid dreamers fail to

---

[21] You must not seek objectifications or anthropomorphizations of God or the divine, but instead, a release of self-identification with the illusory identity in order to surrender into the impersonal consciousness beyond all forms. You are not performing Dream Yoga to find your mental conception and idea of God, but to liberate yourself from all ideas, necessities, and conceptions, until only what is Real is left. Real spirituality is not about mastering meditation, breath control, or lucid dreaming, but about achieving the deathless joy of being eternally happy. And it is by truly waking up that you'll unlock the door toward this ultimate Freedom.

recognize it. People hear a sound and ignore the silence; they see the moon and ignore the space; they watch a movie and forget about the screen; they have a thought and fail to recognize the space between thoughts; even now, you're reading these words and you're not noticing the empty white space that composes the page.

Consciousness of consciousness, in its natural non-dual state, is the goal of Dream Yoga. We can achieve this through the waking state, but for some aspirants, discerning and abiding in the background of consciousness will be more easily achievable in the dream state. From there, it's just a matter of practice until it pervades into the waking state.

> "This world-appearance is experienced only like a day-dream; it is essentially unreal."
>
> - VASISTHA
> VASISTHA'S YOGA

Typically, when you wake up from a dream, regardless of how it was, it's only a matter of seconds, hours, or days until you let go of it and forget about it. You simply drop it, because you recognize it for what it is—"It was just a dream." This is how it will start to occur in the waking state.

As the depth of your consciousness increases, you simply drop your heavy luggage because it no longer belongs to you.

The time where you believed the stories your mind told you about yourself has come to an end. You have broken the hypnotic cycle of the waking dream.

TRANSCENDING BARDO

Some schools of Buddhism believe that by practicing lucid dreaming, you can become awake in *bardo*.

Bardo is an intermediate limbo state that occurs right after death. It's similar to a dream, where some of your subtle desires or deep-rooted traumas manifest and play out until exhausted. This happens so that the individual consciousness can either break free from most of its attachments to the latent impressions gained in this life, or live them out and then move on to its next incarnation.

In the same way that psychological imprints and residual emotions usually carry over from the waking-ego into the creation of the dream-ego and the subsequent dream state, these *vasanas/samskaras* similarly remain present after the death of the physical body and form the transitional state. Unless recognized to be unreal and cleared away during *bardo*, they will also end up forming a new ego—this is the basis for reincarnation and past lives' "seed karma," also known as *Sanchita* karma

Buddhists believe that by practicing lucid dreaming/Dream Yoga during one's lifetime, you train your waking-ego to become conscious during this liminal state. They propose that by continuously becoming lucid during subconscious states, our waking-ego gains the ability to recognize the illusory nature of these dualistic states. Then, once bardo ensues, you'll be able to use this last opportunity—which is similar to a dream—to become lucid and realize your true nature, ending the cycle of reincarnation. Notwithstanding how this sounds, while it may be possible to become aware of your true nature there, it'll also be quite tricky due to the unstable nature of objectivity in subconscious states.

Achieving and stabilizing lucidity, remembering your goal, and realizing your true deathless nature are not easy tasks to accomplish, particularly considering that they must occur during a post-death state that is unknown beforehand. Even though it is similar to a dream state, you don't know how sharp your ability will be at that point, nor how your physical body is going to die. The way you die and the degree of lucidity you have in your final moments also affect the post-death ability to face bardo.

But why wait for death? Why wait for pure consciousness? Why wait for what is never absent? The background of objectless infinite consciousness that is present in bardo is also present right now.

You can become awake while living. Instead of using Dream Yoga to prepare for bardo, you use it to awaken to the pristine unborn consciousness that you already are—through the practice of non-dual Dream Yoga. And if you already are the all-pervading boundless consciousness, you only need to realize it—right here in this lifetime. You don't need to wait for the awareness of being. You just need to be.

CHAPTER 13

THE DROP OF WATER

Deep within the depths of your mind, there is a treasure of incalculable value. But what is this treasure?

Imagine that you are a drop of water and hear rumors of a priceless treasure that lies at the bottom of the ocean. Because you feel incomplete, you, as a small drop of water, embark on a long and arduous journey toward the ocean's bottom to find this supposed treasure that will purportedly liberate you from this feeling of incompleteness.

As you go through your journey, you employ several different techniques and methods, exploring the ocean and its depths. Sometimes you get sidetracked into observing some shoals; other times, your attention is diverted to looking at and playing amongst beautiful corals. These experiences and discoveries are exciting, but you end up forgetting your original purpose and merely keep exploring the marvelous contents of the ocean.

Once you've had enough, you begin to feel incomplete again, and thus you remember your original purpose of going toward the immeasurable treasure that lies at the bottom of the ocean that will supposedly set you free from that feeling once and for all.

A lot of time has passed, and after many detours, forgetfulness, and recommitments, you finally reach the ocean floor. But there's nothing there! You don't see anything, other than some old forgotten rusty mirror. "Was all of this for nothing?!" you ponder, disappointed.

As you grab the mirror, ready to break it in frustration, you look at yourself.

"Wow."

Yes... wow. You can't see yourself.

"Where am I?" you ask. You only see the ocean.

Time seems to freeze as you ponder in disbelief until you realize something:

"I am everywhere. I am not a single drop; I am the whole ocean! I am finally complete—I have always been complete, I just didn't know it!"

This is an excellent story to illustrate lucid dreaming:

You begin your journey because you read or hear about the untold riches of lucid dreaming, and how it can be used as a tool for enlightenment. However, if you get too lost within the dream state (and it is very easy for this to happen) due to its marvelous and alluring life and magic—just like in the ocean—you will forget your true purpose until you suffer and are reminded of what you truly want.

As we dive deeply into lucid dreaming, we should explore the dream state and enjoy its extraordinary contents, but we must never forget that we're ultimately using it as a way to find our inner mirror in order to look at ourselves and realize our inherent oneness and boundlessness.

I want to point out that there are better lucid dreamers than me out there; however, becoming a master at lucid dreaming was not my purpose—and it should not be yours either. Becoming lost on the path of lucid dreaming is something I've seen oneironauts do over and over again. You must use it as a means and not as an end. It is a fun journey, but at some point, you have to transcend it.

Ultimately, lucid dreaming is a tool to become aware of our blissful nature of pure consciousness—a tool for enlightenment. If used with this intention, it is a purposeful spiritual discipline; otherwise, it falls into the same category as most spirituality out there—it becomes the goal instead of the way, transforming itself into a playground for the ego.

It is up to the reader, the dreamer, the practitioner, the seeker, the explorer—to you—to use it to its highest potential.

The Remembered Sadhu

ॐ

I was climbing a mountain trail, close to a jungle. A sense of familiarity hung in the air, but I wasn't sure what it was about. As I was ascending the mountain, the slope was becoming steeper, until it became too precipitous to climb anymore.

"How am I supposed to climb this?", I thought to myself.

Suddenly, I looked down, and saw that I was on a cliff and that there was no trail from where I had just come.

As soon as I realized this, I clung as best as I could to prevent myself from falling, but I really had no way out.

I looked up and saw the sun shining through the clouds, and as I pondered what to do in this life-or-death situation, I saw a hand reaching down from the top of the cliff. I noticed that I was quite close to the top, so I clawed my way up and grabbed that unknown hand, which pulled me to a safe place.

What ensued was quite unexpected, as I astonishedly saw that the hand that saved me belonged a *Sadhvi,* a woman ascetic. I couldn't tell her age, but she wore some of the most beautiful saffron robes I've ever witnessed.

"Look at where you came from," she told me as she pointed to the cliff where I was just moments before. I had just endured the relentless pull of gravity toward an imminent death.

However, as I looked at where she was pointing, I was shocked to find my body still there. "How is it possible that I am still there if I am already here?"

She looked at me and smiled, "You're in a dream."

Instantly, I became lucid, and a blissful energy rose up my spine.

"Your self-image is obsolete; it must die so that you can rebirth into a purer expression. Let yourself fall," said the wise woman.

I took a deep breath, gulped, and embraced death; I let myself fall into the abyss of nothingness.

"Come with me to my cave," said the Sadhvi after I had just observed myself drop into the unknown.

We walked slowly toward an entrance nearby and sat down on a little wooden bench. There was an old stone cooking pot there, filled with boiling water. The whole cave seemed to have been taken out of some ancient eastern parable.

"Tell me, who are you?" I asked while she was busy cooking something in the stone pot.

"I am Maya," the Sadhvi said.

"Maya? Maya, as in the veil, the illusion that prevents everybody from seeing who they really are? Why would Maya help anyone transcend herself?" I asked.

"Yes, that Maya," she said, as I noticed her putting in ingredients to cook a potato and onion soup. "But I don't prevent anyone from seeing themselves—I help them."

"How?" I asked.

"I present to spiritual aspirants what they need to see, at the right time. Many view them as obstacles or seductive illusions, but I'm merely showing them what they need to work on. Maya doesn't trap you—you trap yourself. I merely show you what you need to look at in order to transcend. I am a friend," emphasized Maya.

While I was reflecting on her words, she grabbed two old clay bowls and poured some hot soup in each one.

"Take it, and you will wake up," she said.

I grabbed the bowl, looked at Maya, and asked, "Who was that forgotten Sadhu from my other dream? What did he tell me?"

"Eat the soup," she told me nonchalantly.

Looking into the bowl as I was about to eat the soup, I saw an indistinct face reflected in it. This face constantly seemed to change, just like in the dream I had about the Sadhu.

It was then that it dawned on me: "I am the Sadhu from the other dream!"

It was my own reflection that I was seeing, but it was distorted and continuously changing, so I thought it must be someone else's. But it wasn't. It was me. I am my own Sadhu. What I saw on the river's stream from the other dream was the dynamic aspect of consciousness (Shakti, Divine Feminine). We move through the river of life, continually changing our identity and even body, life after life until we flow into the ocean of immutable Consciousness (Shiva, Divine Masculine). In that river, I saw myself, my journey, and my destination from where I never left.

My body started disintegrating, like pixels being erased from an image. I witnessed this until I had no body left. Then my visual sense disappeared, followed by all of my other senses. I perceived nothing, not even blackness. Soon I had no sense of location, and an enormous wave of bliss and energy began to engulf me. I experienced boundlessness and felt so inexpressibly free, without ground nor sky. I became nothing, everything, and beyond. I was present within absence. How wonderful, a merging of opposites.

The secret key to unlock the mystery of the Self is to find a mirror: a mirror where you can look at yourself and see your true nature. The mirror may be a spiritual practice or discipline such as lucid dreaming, a profound poem, a guru, non-dual pointers, profoundly enlightening words in a book, the sacredness of nature, and so on. Some mirrors are more easily found, and others are better polished; but regardless of the mirror, if you find one, look at it and see yourself, just like the little drop of water. That's all a mirror or reflection does—it shows you what's already there but that you couldn't otherwise see.

I hope this book has shown you a new way to find that mirror. May you see your own reflection in the dance of your own immutable consciousness, and forever melt in the bliss of this knowingness.

If you've enjoyed reading this book and feel that it has made a positive difference in the way you see and approach Lucid Dreaming and Dream Yoga, please show your support by leaving a *Review on the Amazon page*.

It really makes a difference. It helps to spread genuine spiritual teachings to those who are truly seeking them.

May this book plant a powerful seed in your mind, enabling you to experience the dream state as you've never done before. Thank you for reading.

Subscribe and receive the ebook **Uncovering the Real** plus updates and information regarding new books or articles, which will be sent about once or twice a month.

www.RealYoga.info

If you have any doubts or questions regarding this or any of the other books, feel free to contact me at:

Santata@RealYoga.info

SantataGamana's books have gathered over 2000 reviews across all stores with an average rating of 4.5 out of 5 stars.

Read also, by the same author of this book:

— **KRIYA YOGA EXPOSED** [REAL YOGA BOOK #1]

This is not your common guide to Kriya Yoga. It is something you've never seen before. This book brings to light the truth about the current Kriya Yoga Gurus & Organizations. It also contains the explanation of Kriya Yoga techniques, including the Final Special Kriya.

— **THE SECRET POWER OF KRIYA YOGA** [REAL YOGA BOOK #2]

Revealing the fastest Path to Enlightenment. Learn how to fuse Bhakti and Jnana Yoga into Kriya Yoga to unleash the most powerful Yoga ever. After exposing Kriya Yoga in the first volume of this collection, we will now unleash its tremendous power as the basis for all Yogas to come into fruition, going beyond our apparent existence and mortality, into the realmless realms of the Absolute beyond comprehension.

— **KUNDALINI EXPOSED** [REAL YOGA BOOK #3]

Kundalini has been one of the most mysterious and well-kept secrets in the history of spirituality. Not anymore. The book that discloses the Cosmic mystery of Kundalini. The Ultimate Guide to Kundalini Yoga, Kundalini Awakening, Rising, and Reposing on its Hidden Throne.

— **THE YOGA OF CONSCIOUSNESS** [REAL YOGA BOOK #4]

This book contains 25 Direct Practices to Enlightenment. It unveils the ultimate practical guide to Non-Duality (Advaita) and uncovers the unseen blockages made by the ego-mind, in a profound yet accessible way. It goes beyond Spirituality into Awakening Non-Duality.

— **TURIYA: THE GOD STATE** *[REAL YOGA BOOK #5]*

Unravel the ancient mystery of Turiya - The God State. The book that demystifies and uncovers the true state of Enlightened beings. The teachings and expositions in this book are unlike anything you've ever seen. Special paragraphs were written with the underlying purpose of dismantling the illusory constructs that your ego-mind has created.

— **SAMADHI: THE FORGOTTEN EDEN** *[SERENADE OF BLISS BOOK #1]*

Revealing the Ancient Yogic Art of Samadhi. This book unveils the ancient art of how yogis and mystics had the keys to an unlimited reservoir of wisdom and power. It brings the timeless and forgotten wisdom of Samadhi into modern-day practicality.

— **THE YOGIC DHARMA** *[SERENADE OF BLISS BOOK #2]*

Revealing the underlying essence of the Yamas and Niyamas. A profound and unconventional exposition on the spirit of the Yogic Dharma principles. Although they've been distorted to fit today's "self-help chocolate" culture, this book will change that—it will turn your world upside down.

— **TANTRA EXPOSED** *[SERENADE OF BLISS BOOK #4]*

Tantra is a powerful buzzword. But like most buzzwords, it has been misrepresented and bathed in sensationalism, and its original intention and power were forgotten. This book intends to change that. This is the Tantric Resurrection.

All of these books are available @ Amazon as Kindle & Paperback.

GLOSSARY

Asana – Body posture; a sitting pose for spiritual practice.

Background of Consciousness / Awareness – Another name for pure Awareness. However, such a name presupposes that there is a foreground or that which is witnessed, implying a duality. That's quite right, but it should be understood that this name is a helpful clue for seekers because it helps them take a step back from the mental contents with which they are usually identified, so that they can repose in awareness itself.

Beingness – The intrinsic nature of consciousness is "Being." To be is to be conscious. At first, "Beingness" might be felt as a profound experience of stillness, peace, joy, etc., but as one goes further, it will dissolve our individuality, and our blissful Oneness will shine through.

Chakra – Wheel/plexus, a psychic-energy center.

Dream-ego/self/consciousness – The consciousness with which you experience the non-lucid dream state. When lucid, the waking-ego replaces the dream-ego.

Dream Yogi – A lucid dreamer that uses their dreams for spiritual purposes.

Ego – "I," the thought "I" or "I-ego." It is the erroneous belief of being a separate being or entity. For a more in-depth understanding, refer to *The Yoga of Consciousness*.

Enlightenment – The realization of your true nature/original state of unbounded happiness and peace; Self-realization; Nirvana; Mukti; Refer to the *Real Yoga Series* for a comprehensive explanation.

God – God is neither male nor female. God is not a person or an entity—that would make God limited. God is the all-pervading Consciousness, being formless, timeless, and unborn. It is the infinite Awareness that each one of us possesses, and out of which everything is "made."

Kundalini – The primal spiritual energy said to be located at the base of the spine. Cosmic Kundalini is the same energy but rather than being the individual's latent energy, it is the universal latent energy, being infinitely more powerful.

Lucid Dreamer – A lucid dreamer refers to anyone who becomes lucid in a dream, regardless of their purpose, which, more often than not, is not spiritual advancement. On the other hand, a dream yogi is someone who intends to use lucid dreams as a path toward enlightenment.

Mantra – Sacred syllable or word or set of words.

Maya – The veil of illusion that appears to cover our true infinite nature. This veil allows pure empty consciousness to believe it has divided itself into many different forms, each with different qualities, from beings to thoughts to galaxies. It is the **manifested relative**: the contents of Awareness which have manifested from its infinite potential.

Non-duality or **Non-dual state** – "Not two;" i.e., a stateless state where only consciousness blissfully aware of itself exists; the end of the dichotomy of "I" and "other." The original natural state of being. Non-duality cannot be truly described in a glossary; refer to *Turiya – The God State*.

Oneironaut – A lucid dreamer.

Parvastha – The "After-Kriya" blissful Self-Awareness state.

Prana – Life-force.

Pranayama – Life-force restraint/control technique.

Pure Consciousness – Our pure and true formless Self-aware nature. That which is conscious; Is your body conscious? No. Is your brain conscious? No. We could go on all day, until we realize that nothing is conscious by itself, except consciousness. I use Consciousness and Awareness interchangeably throughout this book.

REM – Rapid eye movement sleep is a phase of sleep distinguished by the rapid movement of the eyes. It is the best state to experience vivid dreams and lucid dreams.

Sadhana – Spiritual Practice.

Sadhu – A male spiritual ascetic; Sadhvi is a female ascetic.

***Sanchita* Karma** – The store of our past karmas [actions] that are yet to be experienced.

Self – With a capital "S" means pure consciousness or pure Awareness, devoid of any objects; self with a small "s" is synonymous with ego or "I."

Sense of Being – Presence or awareness of existing/of being/of the background of consciousness/of that which is aware; Kriya Yoga's Parvastha.

Shakti - Personification of Kundalini, the life-force principle that gives life to the Universe.

Subconscious mind – That which is beneath the conscious mind. Sometimes, it is also called the "unconscious."

Vasanas / Samskaras – Latent tendencies, recollections, or mental impressions stored in the causal body, responsible for reincarnation.

Waking-ego/self/consciousness – The consciousness with which you experience wakefulness. A "modulation" of pure consciousness; the conscious mind.

Printed in Great Britain
by Amazon